HIGHWAY	—— ROAD	┼┼┼┼┼ RAIL	├———┤ CABLEWAY
FRONTIER	······· PATH	■ COL	△ MAIN PEAKS

TOUR OF MONT BLANC

The Aiguille Verte seen from the Flégère path

TOUR OF MONT BLANC

by
Andrew Harper

*Illustrations by the author
except where otherwise stated*

CICERONE PRESS
MILNTHORPE, CUMBRIA

© Andrew Harper 1997
ISBN 1 85284 240 7
First published 1977, 2nd Edition 1982
3rd Edition 1988, Reprinted 1991
4th Edition 1997, Revised reprint 2000

When I first went to Chamonix and looked over the Mer de Glace towards the barrier wall out of which rise the Grandes Jorasses and the Aig. du Géant, the landscape appeared to get worse in its ruggedness and foreboding. Such was my impression that I felt nothing could lay beyond, unless it be further desolation.

I have long since realised that this same barrier actually forms the frontier with Italy. Courmayeur lies just to the south - similar to Chamonix in many respects - the two being separated by ten miles of grandeur.

Around the massif of Mont Blanc lies a chain of seven main valleys through which a thread of fine footpaths take the wanderer on a circuit of eye-opening awe. These paths link with each other to form the *TOUR OF MONT BLANC*.

CONTENTS

Advice to Readers

Readers are advised that whilst every effort is taken by the author to ensure the accuracy of this guidebook, changes can occur which may affect the contents. A book of this nature with detailed descriptions and detailed maps is more prone to change than a more general guide. Waymarking alters, there may be new buildings or eradication of old buildings. It is advisable to check locally on transport, accommodation, shops etc. but even rights of way can be altered, paths can be eradicated by landslip, forest clearances or changes of ownership. The publisher would welcome notes of any such changes.

FOREWORD

With the publication of this 4th edition the opportunity has been taken to include detail relating to several significant alterations to the facilities in the area. Perhaps the most notable change has been the commissioning of the long-promised *Elena* refuge which occupies a very strategic and prestigious position towards the head of the Italian val Ferret, giving scope for greater flexibility in the staging of that section of the route.

For those contemplating their first alpine walking venture, be assured that many have made their first paces on this circuit and enjoyed the whole experience. As will be emphasised in the following pages, the major prerequisite is to attain a suitable level of fitness and to prepare for the enterprise by practising long-distance hill-walking on home ground, eventually with a rucksack filled and weighted to represent the load you expect to take when the time comes to set off.

It is an unfortunate practicality that a book such as this has to be compartmentalised into 'stages' and these might not coincide with the rate at which you want to progress the route. You must adjust your staging to suit your own capabilities, never feeling that there is an obligation to go further on any day just to tie in with the proposals put forward in my chapters. Certain landfalls will have to be made in order to secure accommodation for the night, but you will quickly be able to sense what your limits will be and attune yourself accordingly.

Some of the advice I give might already be known to you and, after all, a lot is only common sense. You might even disagree with or take exception to some of my opinions! Having been an avid alpine walker for many years I find that there are still things that I can learn to advantage, so I hope you will accept my suggestions in the spirit they are intended and - most important of all - enjoy your holiday in *the Mont Blanc area* to the full.

So, assuming you didn't buy this book just because of the pretty picture on the front cover, then the countdown to one of your very best holiday experiences begins *right here.*

Andrew Harper - 1997

INTRODUCTION

The 'official' *Tour du Mont Blanc* (abbreviated: 'TMB') follows an established route around the main block of mountains containing not only Mont Blanc but its principal allied summits such as Verte, Chardonnet, Goûter, Géant, Jorasses, d'Argentière, Dolent and numerous others.

The author has walked the Tour several times in the traditional 'anti-clockwise' direction, once 'clockwise' and made numerous incursions into the region. There are several alternative routes that subsequently link and there are no two organisations that are in complete agreement as to the paths that should be followed. The route described in this book, along with suggestions for alternative exploration, has been created on what the author thinks gives the very best perspective and appreciation of the whole region and provides the best balance of visual return for the physical effort required. At the end of each day there should be a body with healthy appetite, a thirst and a readiness for sleep that is balanced by a feeling of satisfaction and accomplishment. At every opportunity recommendations are made that will bring the walker into closer contact with the area and enhance memories of the visit.

The 'general information' section is intended to provide all the useful detail that will permit easier preparation and planning for the venture, intending to allay a whole range of problems that can beset most people, particularly those heading for their first Alpine experience.

The author has chosen the start/finish point at les Houches for several reasons. It is the nearest point on the circuit for those coming to the area from Britain. This is true for the sea/rail routes as well as those coming by car. Those using air travel will invariably select Geneva as the nearest airport and the onward journey from there will either be by coach or train and come to the same north-west corner at which les Houches lies. Starting the walk from here provides an early glimpse over the lovely Chamonix valley, a more leisurely and closer study of which can be made at the very end of the holiday, efficiently absorbing any 'days in hand'.

Some may argue that the approach to Martigny is to be preferred and, of course, this is a sensible alternative. Travellers by rail via Paris might find this spot more accessible and there may be fare concessions that dictate the choice. However, the first-time visitors are encouraged to commence at les Houches as the author believes that the vista unfolds in better sequence from there and the grading or 'stride' will generally be found to develop more agreeably.

A word about the timings. These relate to the pace expected from experienced *slow-to-moderate* fell walkers. It allows for momentary halts to appreciate the scenery, regain breath or consult the map. Beyond that, the time absorbed by photography, shopping, eating, prolonged sightseeing and the like must be added. The times should only be a guide and will vary enormously from party to party, person to person, day to day. Bad weather invariably adds to the hours, the pace then being determined by an attempt to limit the condensation within the rainwear.

The **cols** (passes) that will be found in progressing the TMB are, by their very nature, amongst the highest places that will be encountered along the way. As such, and without exception, they offer superb vantage points where one can linger, relax and savour the scenic grandeur. The challenge - if it *is a challenge* - will be in getting up to them where the vistas they afford usually more than compensate for any exertion and, what's more, it'll be all downhill and easier on the other side.

All the timings were measured by the author with a chronometer on one of his visits during which an 11kg (24lb) pack was carried with the exception of the Saleina defile/d'Orny hut/col de la Breya route where the times quoted are approximations.

One final tip: EXPECT bad weather and if it comes then you won't feel so bad about it; you will then be able to regard GOOD weather as a bonus! This philosophy is probably the best advice that could be given.

GENERAL INFORMATION

When to go

Based on personal experience and reports given to the author by other people, it seems that the likelihood of troublesome snow laying as late as early July determines the first time that the Tour can be commenced.

Many people have been known to go earlier and found the passes relatively easy to cross, whereas a few going at the end of August have been unfortunate in encountering unusual snowfall; there are no guarantees! The difference between these two extremes is that persistent snow in June does not clear readily, whereas freak snow in August is just as likely to clear in the time it took to fall.

The days are long in July but the weather conditions are notoriously wet. August tends to be humid and muggy but the first three weeks are to be avoided because the French vacation period will be at its peak. During this time the hills are well subscribed with these holiday-makers, adding to your vocabulary if you are studying the language; however, it will be with these same folk that you will be competing for the limited accommodation at the night stops. They thin out by about the 20th, so if you go then and spread into September there may be benefits derived from the low-season charges made by the hotels which appear to come into force on the 1st of that month.

Daylight gets effective about 7.00am and it gets dark by 8.30pm in early September, so the days are still long enough. The weather seems more settled, too. Alpine flowers will have gone through their best period, but plenty are left to provide pleasure and to give some colour. The end of September through to mid-October can have its rewards, although the autumn shades hardly establish themselves fully until mid-November. At that time of year one can walk all day and not see a soul and this is ideal if it is solitude that is wanted. The penalty for such a late visit will be that the majori of refuges will be closed.

No mention has been made so far in relation to the animal life that exists in the region. Birds seem small in number, although eagle-like predators can occasionally be seen soaring in the thermals.

An idyllic scene in a remote area: the vallée des Glaciers near Chapieux

Some of the passes are habitual crossing places for migrating birds each autumn and spring, ornithologists being alert to this phenomenon. The three types of mountain deer do not all seem to be represented in the area, only the small chamois (like the 'Babycham' advert) seems to have the run of the hillsides. The beaver-like and lovable marmot is undoubtedly the character you are likely to come across more than any other: probably the first you will know of their proximity is when you hear a shrill whistle, startling if at close quarters. This call will be from the sentry who can usually be seen on a highish position where he warns his fellows of impending danger. The long, sleek, ermine is in the area but like all of the other animals they are unlikely to be seen at all unless you show an avid interest and scan the hillsides for indications of their presence.

Summing up, then: 20th August to 15th September has, on average, all the advantages although the author is aware that this is at the tail-end of the summer and those with a streak of impatience might not want to wait until then for their holiday. The summer months ought to be used for practice walks in hilly terrain and to

11

gradually become familiar with new equipment. This kind of training usually pays handsome dividends, especially for those who are preparing for their Alpine début.

How to get there

1. *By air to Geneva, then continuing by train to St. Gervais*

The connection from the airport to the railway station serving St. Gervais seems rather complicated but is not all that difficult. Bus outside the railway station entrance at Geneva airport: No.10 to Bel Air (down by the river: a 15min ride). The ticket is acquired from a machine adjacent to the bus stop (if change is needed then a note can be exchanged at the railway booking office just down the escalator). It is necessary to get another bus, No.12, which operates along a main road which is second back from the river and goes in the left direction, boardable on the other side of the road. Alight at 'gare des Eaux-Vives' (all the stops are named, so it is easy to follow the progress of the bus and anticipate when the Eaux-Vives stop is next): about a 15min ride. After alighting from the bus, the railway terminus is situated up a street on the LHS. Note that the bus ticket has a set time validity from the moment it is first used which should suffice for both legs of the journey to Eaux-Vives.

At Eaux-Vives buy a ticket to les Houches, a return or single as required. It might be necessary to change at Annemasse and la Roche-sur-Foron but the travelling ticket inspector will probably speak enough English to confirm this. St. Gervais is the terminus for the normal-gauge train and a narrow-gauge train heading for Chamonix is the one required for continuing to les Houches and, once on the way, it takes about 30mins. The journey is full of interest and excitement increases as Mont Blanc is approached with stupendous views from the carriage windows.

A taxi from the airport would take away all the trauma of the bus journey within Geneva, but, although expensive, it becomes more economical when there is more than one person. As the trains from Eaux-Vives are infrequent, a taxi might make just that essential difference in making the connection.

2. *Travel to Paris, either by air or the established cross-channel routes then by train to St. Gervais*

From the French capital there are generally two departures per day to St. Gervais, one leaving in the early morning to arrive late afternoon. The other is an overnight service which delivers its passengers at St. Gervais about 8.00am where an awaiting connection reaches les Houches around 8.30am., so one could step from the train and immediately begin to enjoy a full alpine day. Faster TGV trains are speeding things up and are being rostered to get closer and closer to Chamonix.

3. *Train from Paris to Martigny by mainline*

This route is comparable in time and cost to the St. Gervais approach but as the years progress different discount structures for the tourist traveller might influence the choice of route on the grounds of expenditure. Getting to Martigny from Paris certainly seems quicker when compared to the wholly French routing, but, here again, the continuing policy of extension to the relatively new TGV high-speed train system might alter the balance in the near future. Train timings and costs will have to be the subject of enquiry and scrutiny prior to making your reservations. Be alert to some odd discount structures - for example, the day of the week on which the journey commences *within* France can influence the discount available.

As far as train journeys are concerned, the route to Martigny is more straightforward than the one towards St. Gervais, which currently has many changes of direction to contend with and, at night, the association of annoying shunting activity. Martigny is further from the TMB circuit, though, which would have to be joined at either Champex, la Forclaz or possibly col des Montets. Linking train to Orsières then bus for Champex: bus from station forecourt of Martigny station for la Forclaz: narrow-gauge train from Martigny station to Vallorcine then a pleasant $1^{1/2}$ hour walk over the pastures to join the TMB circuit at col des Montets.

4. *By coach*

Probably the cheapest method of reaching the area is to make use of the 'Eurolines' service operating from Victoria coach station in London. Details will be available from their main office at 52 Grosvenor Gardens, London, SW1 (Tel: 01582 404511 or any National Express enquiry centre). Departures seem to be at 3.00pm arriving

Life on the TMB: old transport customs die hard. A scene near Contamines

about noon the following day. An even cheaper fare is possible for members of the British Mountaineering Council, details of which are available from that organisation. (The recognised stop is Chamonix, so unless an agreement has been made for a 'drop' at les Houches, it will be necessary to return that short distance by either the train or the local bus.)

5. By personal transport

These approaches will show the les Houches corner as being nearest. Car owners will have the responsibility of leaving their vehicle until returning to it some two weeks later. Coming to some arrangement with a garage or hotel might be the solution rather than to leave it completely unattended. The Bellevue campsite in les Houches appears to offer a service by allowing a car to be placed in a compound. Another place that appears to permit an extended parking facility is the hotel at Forclaz and their reservation desk would be the place to enquire. Chamonix has a long-term multistorey car park in the centre of the town, secured at night: *Parking Couvert de Chamonix Sud.*

14

Currency

Progressing through three countries means that appropriate currencies will have to be carried. More ground is covered in the French sectors compared with either Italy or Switzerland and, particularly if the journey to the area is to be made over land, this dictates the need for more French money than any other. Arrival by air at Geneva will immediately drum up the need for some Swiss francs for the bus/taxi and the cost of the rail fare from Eaux-Vives to les Houches. Maybe *Gaz* is required, a meal or an overnight hotel?

Travellers' cheques are a useful adjunct to any money carried. The opportunity to cash them is limited to the main villages where the banks have strange hours of opening, although there are bureaux de change/cambio which are of far greater service and where the transaction is speedy by comparison. Most Tourist Offices also appear to have the facility to change cheques. Smaller denominations can often be cashed at a hotel or garage where the rate of exchange is not all that unfavourable.

VISA, ACCESS and other credit cards are hesitantly accepted but, surprisingly, some hotels in the region will not accept them as a form of payment. If you intend to pay by this method you ought first to make enquiries as to their validity.

The *Eurocheque* scheme is spreading in popularity, facilitating guaranteed cheque payments in addition to providing an additional source for obtaining funds from its associated cashpoints. Your bank will be able to advise.

Insurance

In keeping to the main paths you will stand little chance of coming to grief, although the ankle is always at risk. With so much rock making up the environment it must be acknowledged that there is some slight danger of a boulder bounding towards you: even stones dislodged by some careless or thoughtless individual on a higher path can have painful consequences. Whilst the odds are in your favour for completing the Tour without mishap, injuries do occur. Hospitalisation and medical care cost a lot of money, so for this reason you should consider taking out some form of holiday insurance. Ascertain that there is no clause which will absolve

15

liability for policyholders engaged in mountaineering pursuits. When you get the policy, it is advisable to leave a photostat with a relative or friend and take the original with you.

For British walkers there are reciprocal rights available under the National Health Service arrangements, but it will be necessary to approach your DHSS office to get details. This might result in you being issued with a form E111 and the first thing you have to do is to get a photostat, taking *both* with you on the holiday (it's in the small print!).

In the section dealing with mountain safety you will be encouraged to take a whistle but before actually using it to summon assistance do give very careful thought as to whether such a call need be made. Blowing whistles on mountainsides can be **extremely** expensive: the person being aided will subsequently have to bear all the costs of the rescue operation and the thought of this should be sufficient justification for getting adequate insurance cover. Ordinary holiday insurance does **not** cover mountain rescue but special policies are available for UK citizens only from:

British Mountaineering Council, 177/179 Burton Road, West Didsbury, Manchester M20 2BB. Tel: 0161 445 4747 (Available to members only)

See also the outdoor press for other companies.

Basic Precautions for Mountain Safety

Ensure that you have adequate, warm clothing.

Plan your day carefully, not over-estimating your physical ability. Take into account the limitations imposed by the weakest or least experienced member of the party as well as being vigilant for anyone who might be showing signs of approaching ill-health or fatigue.

Endeavour to obtain weather forecasts - ask refuge guardians or make enquiries from the police for their opinion about the prospects before setting off. Keep an eye open for indications of worsening weather and be alert to the prospect of mist closing in with little warning.

Don't hesitate to turn back or cut a section from your itinerary if the weather deteriorates. Pressing on is folly and has led to disastrous - even fatal - results. Don't think that just because you have gone beyond the halfway mark of a route that it will be easier to continue: returning might be longer in distance but it will at least negotiate familiar territory and you will have knowledge of the accommodation available. Incidentally, it is always good advice to make a mental note of possible places to stay or shelter as you progress - you never know when you might be glad to make use of them should you have to return.

It might prove helpful to consult the refuge guardian, police or even the hotelier by telling them where you intend to go. They are better placed to know about the state of the paths and give advice, although the language barrier might be a hindrance. One of the best sources of information will be people who are walking the route in the opposite direction - they are in the best position of all to advise and for this reason alone it often pays to have a chat with them as they pass.

Keep to the approved paths, staying together as a group and accept all the decisions made by the leader. Think ahead and make some plans for a rendezvous place and time should you get parted: even when separating to visit shops in the villages it can be extremely frustrating and time wasting if there is some difficulty in re-uniting.

Know what to do in an emergency by reading such publications as *First Aid for Hillwalkers and Climbers* (Cicerone Press).

Never venture onto glaciers until you have first learned the special and necessary techniques.

Fatigue or slight injury can delay or halt progress and may mean a night in the open on high ground with attendant risk of exposure. The risk can be lessened to a large degree by carrying a survival bag, although if you find yourself without one a conventional dodge is to empty your rucksack and then draw it up over feet and legs. Put on all the clothing you can at an early stage and aim to keep the extremities (head, hands and feet) as warm as possible. Take the best advantage of any shelter that may avail itself, getting into a position that offers the best protection from any wind.

For those who disregard precautions, the onset of bad weather can mean acute physical discomfort, loss of direction, growing fear and even collapse. The surest defence against these dangers is the observance of all the mountain safety procedures.

17

*A Swiss frontier guard at the col du Grand Ferret. In the background
the Grandes Jorasses*

Should you want to summon assistance then the recognised signalling pattern is by whistle, lamp or voice. Six long blasts, flashes or yells for one minute, followed by one minute of silence. Then repeat. The spaces of each alternate minute are to permit a reply which will consist of three blasts.

This list of precautions would not be complete without reminding you about the value of the compass. Carrying one is not an effective answer unless you've acquainted yourself in how it should be used. One of the best applications is to continually up-date its setting for the general direction of travel, particularly if mist threatens. An indispensable item.

It is a sign of the times that river waters are held back as part of the hydro-electric schemes and that is why some of the rivers are, at the limit, devoid of water. Occasionally water is released from these catchments at an enormous rate and becomes a danger. At several places on the TMB you will see warnings of flash floods so be careful not to venture onto a river bed if these notices are on display.

The Refuges

Newcomers to the mountains are often uncertain as to the formalities involved in gaining access to the refuges. Membership of an organisation is not essential although there are advantages such as reduction in charges and priority of admission but if the only aim is to save money then the savings are not likely to outweigh the expense of joining.

The refuges all tend to have their own character and a lot depends on the personality of the guardian who sometimes takes residence with his family for the season. At a lot of them, all the produce used in supplying the meals has to be carried up from the valley by the guardian although an increasing use is being made of helicopter drops for this purpose. However, be tolerant of a restricted menu. At some refuges the guardian might only prepare a meal if the major ingredient (meat or whatever) is given to him by the visitor.

Towards the end of the season you may even find a refuge unattended so allow for this eventuality by carrying at the least some soup powder. There is normally provision made for self-cooking and an area set aside for this: usually with pans, crockery and cutlery. A small fee is charged for the use of this facility.

The basic sleeping arrangement found in the refuges has dormitory style bedding where mattresses are laid side-by-side with a pillow and two blankets allocated to each space. The sexes are not usually segregated. Some people used to the routine take their own sheet to separate them from the supplied blankets but, unlike the YHA, its use is not obligatory. Keep your torch handy so that any move from the bedspace during the hours of darkness can be managed through the heap of rucksacks, pitons, crampons, ice-axes, sticks and discarded clothing. You will notice that boots were not included in the list: they would have been compulsorily deposited in the entrance lobby, where ungainly plastic plimsolls are available to the visitor.

Few premises have bedrooms as such, but quite often the dormitory accommodation is divided into rooms of varying size. Obviously, the smaller number of people sleeping in any one room will increase the likelihood of an undisturbed night. Bunk beds are a familiar feature, where the restless occupant usually influences the slumbers of the other!

It would seem that the guardians each have authority to end their season depending on the circumstances and fall in demand. Always be prepared to find a refuge closed, even though being assured otherwise as you passed through the preceding village. In such an eventuality, don't overlook the strong likelihood of a winter room being open; access might be through an unimposing door you might otherwise not be tempted to open. Bare necessities would then be available and payment - however little - must subsequently be made in the next valley or at the next refuge.

It is very difficult to make reservations in advance and even if this is achieved a booking will not be held for an extremely late arrival. A disadvantage with booking is surely that the walker is tied to making a particular landfall each day - possibly running the danger of outreaching his capabilities. Far better to have flexibiiity of manoeuvre and allow the odd day tolerance for rest, sightseeing or to sit out bad weather without being under an obligation to press on. The best way, really, is to proceed as far as you feel able each day, aiming to arrive at a place where accommodation is reckoned to be available. Arriving early is the best way to guarantee a place, but finding the refuge full to the seams with a school party can come as a rude shock, although you would probably be squeezed in somehow.

Gîtes d'Étape

A gîte is the French name to describe a shepherd's cottage but a *gîte d'étape* is a different thing entirely. It is a small and inexpensive place to stay and it seems as though encouragement is made to use it as a transit lodging place rather than for a prolonged stay. They seem to be springing up in quantity in the Alps and to have been created from, say, a disused barn by the villagers who care for the passer-by to the extent of providing adequate shelter, toilet and washing facilities. There might be a selfish reason behind the policy of providing these places; obviously the rambler with all of his dust and wet clothing is steered away from the more expensive hotels to leave them uncluttered and available for the motorist trade.

Be on the lookout for these as they can be superb. They are similar in many ways to the *dortoir*.

Dortoirs

The literal translation of the word means dormitory.

These are rooms either in a building built for the purpose or in an attic or outbuilding at an hotel where bedding and washing/toilet facilities exist at very reasonable prices. A hotelier might not disclose the availability of such a room if he still has expensive bedrooms to allocate so the phrase *'avez-vous le dortoir, s'il vous plait?'* can often produce a room which might not otherwise have been offered.

Other Places to Stay

Lists of accommodation can be obtained by corresponding with the local Tourist Offices, but delay your enquiry until early April as an earlier approach may bring forth their winter tariffs complete with unwanted information about their ski holidays. Should you write abroad, then it is courteous (but not always necessary) to send an International Reply Coupon with the enquiry, these being available at all Post Offices: certainly there would be a better chance of getting a reply.

It is reassuring to have a hotel list in your hand for the odd occasion when you stride into a town late one evening. Providing you can reach the Tourist Office before it closes - about 7.00pm usually - then they will be able to sense your requirements on the spot and tell you what is available, often saving a needless search at the end of a tiring day. Even when closed, some Offices have the hotel situation displayed outside their premises to facilitate selection. At the extreme, the effects of a bad choice will only last one night; it's not as though you will be committing yourself to a fortnight's stay.

Generally speaking the following places are thriving resorts and therefore have plenty of spaces from which a choice can be made:

Chamonix, Courmayeur, les Houches, les Contamines, Argentière, Champex, Orsières, Martigny, St. Gervais.

Whilst there are hotels, their number is strictly limited at:

la Vachey, les Chapieux, Ferret, la Fouly, Praz de Fort, Forclaz, le Tour, Dolonne, Verrand, Entrèves, la Palud, Planpincieux, Tresse.

Hotels are obliged to display the costs of a room and this notice is generally to be found pinned to the inside of bedroom doors. It is quite common to find bedrooms equipped for two persons with the price quoted per room and it may be found that a stay under these conditions will prove economical. If your aim is to save money then don't have the preconceived idea that older places offer the best terms - quite often the author has been impressed by the reasonable tariffs exacted by the more modern establishments and certainly the facilities are a step-up from the older places. On the other hand, older places can have a charm of their own; the fitted bathroom is not everything!

At a hotel, the so-called *continental* breakfast is not usually included in the price: nor is it always compulsory, although some managements like to give the impression that it is. At many places it is not available until 8.00am - later on Sundays - and a valuable part of the day will have been lost in waiting for it. You may well consider it to be far better to obtain a fresh loaf from the local shops and to enjoy this with a brew-up after making some progress.

It is normal to hand in passports when registering at each place of stay, but the practice is not consistent. Should you be asked to do this then take the greatest care in remembering to collect it before departure. Quite often you will be asked to complete a simple questionnaire: a statutory requirement, but a nuisance all the same. Whatever else you do, insist on settling the hotel bill before retiring to bed as this will save a needless wait in the morning until a responsible member of the management puts in an appearance.

A comprehensive Accommodation Directory is appended at the rear of this book.

Backpacking

This form of travel has a lot to recommend it, overcoming the need to make certain landfalls each night in order to secure traditional accommodation. It follows from this that there could be a more efficient way of dividing the Tour. Backpacking is the answer when there is no accommodation, but the Mont Blanc area is adequately served with places to stay at conveniently spaced intervals. So, don't invest in backpacking equipment just for the sake of it as the penalty of increased weight may be the price you pay for making the TMB into an exercise of labour rather than that of enjoyment.

Pitching tents above the tree line seems to raise no objection from the authorities in France and Italy, although recognised sites should be used when lower down. Switzerland is stricter when dealing with the camper and, generally speaking, camping at other than official sites is forbidden. The author generally prefers to take his tent and sleep in that for the majority of nights, only using the occasional refuge or hotel when foul weather or other reasons influence the decision. The essential *Karrimat* is a curse to stow (witness every other hiker who is carrying one) and it will be a day to applaud when a rucksack manufacturer actually acknowledges that these awkward things have to be carried and make some practical provision in their design for stowing the things.

Sleeping Bags

Established backpackers will already have their favourite brand of bag, chosen as much for its packed size and weight as its thermal insulation. But - if you're not backpacking - do you really need one? Gîtes d'étape and dortoirs tend to be at lower altitudes than the refuges, but, even in these, it can sometimes get miserably cold and there are bound to be times when you wish you had that little bit of extra protection to snuggle into. Just think of the situation in a crowded refuge where there is absolutely no alternative than to sleep on the floor of the entrance lobby (a not unheard of experience, particularly when atrocious weather drives a mountainside's-worth of hikers into the one place!). It is a very useful thing to have one on the TMB and if you decide to make a purchase be prepared to pay a little extra to get one that packs small and will be light to carry, notwithstanding that you will have it for many such holidays to come.

If you are contemplating joining a guided tour, then you could discover that the organisers might stipulate the need of taking a sleeping bag as a condition of participation.

Clothing and Gear

There is one basic difference to be acknowledged between fellwalking in Britain and handling the route described in this book: the temperature can change by as much as 20°C in as many minutes, the effect of which is made much worse by a vanishing sun. This would be an extreme occurrence but you should at least be aware of the possibility. The author hopes that your Tour will be free of bad weather with continual clear visibility but such perfection is rare and you must be prepared for the worst conditions as they present themselves. The paths are quite often the highest paths in the area and with increased height it can be assumed that the dangers associated with bad weather will increase also.

So, take warm clothing such as thick shirts, substantial breeches or trousers, a windproof jacket or anorak, woollen cap (one that can be turned down over the ears), socks or stockings in good condition. Denim jeans are considered quite unsuitable in bad weather. They are also generally too tight fitting. Gloves will often come in useful and waterproof overgloves are advantageous as they basically reduce the effects of a chilling wind although their main purpose is to repel rain or snow. Mountain walkers often prefer to take two thin pullovers so that they can be donned or removed according to the needs of the moment rather than the popular 'all or nothing' chunky sweater.

Boots are a must and the selection of these will be based on individual preference - they must not only be waterproof but be in a state of good repair (don't forget to take a spare lace!). Make certain there is plenty of room for the toes and that they fit snugly at the ankle (exactly half of the Mont Blanc Tour is downhill and it is the fit of the boots that stops the toes holding back the complete bodyweight). Of course, new boots must be 'run in' prior to departure and any adjustments made in good time. You will need to take a pair of trainers for the hotels and evenings - at most refuges the wearing of soft-soled shoes is a regulation.

Footcare is a delicate subject to voice, but struggling to walk on a blistered foot can have the effect of holding back other companions as well as registering pain with each successive pace. Washing the feet thoroughly every evening is a hygienic duty that many choose to shun and it is understandably all too easy to cut corners at the end of an exhausting day. Practically everyone the author has spoken to who is seen to be suffering in this way admits that they had not given their feet this simple and worthwhile attention. No more will be said on the topic.

Anklets can come in handy, their main service being to reject small stones entering the boot. Leggings are really not necessary but can be a blessing if there is the odd stretch of deep fresh snow to wade through. Ropes will not be needed, nor crampons, although some people find the prospect of taking an ice-axe comforting. If you feel that you can come to terms with a walking stick then this can really come into its own and be a worthy companion.

Rainwear in the form of a waterproof cagoule or jacket plus over-trousers is a most important prerequisite but don't get the impression that it is all dark skies and thunder: sunglasses will probably get far more use! A brimmed cap will help overcome the problems when the weather shows its more cheerful self and good quality glacier cream should be applied to the lips, nose and tops of the ears as a prevention rather than cure. A thin summer shirt will make the hot days more tolerable.

The rucksack should ideally be of such a capacity that it just comfortably holds the *maximum* you wish to carry that is not actually being worn. Don't plan to strap your jacket on the outside but make sure there will be room for it within. Too loose a rucksack can be uncontrollable and a nuisance. Side pockets are useful for water carrying and small items on general call such as film cans, ointments, washing gear and the like. Aim to keep it as light in weight as possible to the point of being ruthless. Remember that whatever style of pack you decide upon, it will be with you for every pace of the Tour, so don't be hurried into buying a design that is not going to be wholly suited to your needs. Getting a waterproof cover for it might be a good investment.

A little washing powder will be useful, but having washed your clothes it becomes a problem to dry them thoroughly. A good idea is to take a few safety pins and use them to fasten the items onto the outside of the rucksack as you march along. Take a modest-sized torch, such that the battery stands an even chance of outliving

Life on the TMB: in Courmayeur there is still a communal washing place for those who want it

frequent short bursts of use. Another useful thing to take is a foam rubber cushion (about 8x12x1$^{1}/_{2}$ inches), covered in thin material: this will act as an additional pillow in the refuges and take the sting out of lunchbreak rests and could help to protect your camera when it is in your rucksack.

Finally in this list of suggestions - plenty of thin plastic bags. These will be useful for all kinds of food, not only keeping perishable foods fresh for longer but saving the other contents in the rucksack from contamination by spilt liquids, split tomatoes, etc. Bread will 'survive' for days if additionally placed in a large polythene bag. Wrapping clothes in these bags has double value: preventing dampness reaching dry things as well as giving neater and smaller items to stow.

Water and Cookers

You will surely take a water container and this will become part of your lifeline for days on end. It will be of additional comfort if it is designed so that you can drink directly from it and has an efficient screw cap which does not leak. Make sure you fill it up before leaving your hotel/refuge, although you will encounter numerous standpipes. If the water is unsuitable, then there is usually a prominently placed notice to that effect: *l'eau non potable*. Most of the streams seem harmless enough, but you will have to make your own decision about that. There are proprietary tablets available that can be added to the water - these seem to work on the basis of chlorination. If having added them you cannot taste the chlorine then you must add another until you do.

A small butane cooker will be of value in brewing-up for tea, coffee and the occasional soup. One 190gm cartridge per person per fortnight seems to be the way it works out, providing an effective attempt has been made to screen the flame. The screw-top self-sealing type does not appear to be available over there, whereas the pierceable *Gaz* is on sale readily both in the 190gm and 90gm sizes. If you are travelling by air, be cautioned that the conveyance of these cartridges is **strictly forbidden** whether or not they have been pierced.

The cartridges are on general sale throughout the region, so they are easy to acquire. For those passing through Geneva, *Gaz* can be obtained from the sports section of the department store *Placette* which is in the centre of the city.

The Languages

Three countries are involved in the TMB. French is the language spoken in the part belonging to France of course and it also happens to be the natural tongue of the people in the Swiss section. In the Italian section many residents regard French as their second language.

There is a general claim that 'they all speak English' but this has not been the author's experience. Very few speak English to an acceptable degree of competence, so maybe it is up to us to bridge the gap by an attempt to study the basics of *their* language before we venture abroad.

Maps

The main need for a map is to provide names of the sighted points of interest. Unless visibility is poor, they will not be needed on a moment-to-moment basis for route finding but certainly come into their own during the planning stage.

Institut Géographique National (IGN)
1:25,000 In two sheets: 3630 O - Chamonix & Massif du Mont Blanc
3531 E - St. Gervais-les-Bains

Their 'blue' series is the standard map with excellent detail, but the slightly more expensive 'TOP 25' versions 3630 O. T and 3531 E. T include additional walking and tourist information.

Didier & Richard
1:50,000 In one sheet: No.8 - Mont Blanc & Beaufortin

Should you encounter difficulty in obtaining these maps locally, then the following specialists will normally be in a position to supply:

View down the val de Montjoie over the chalets de Balme (Stage 2)
(Photo: R.B. Evans)

Looking back to the col du Bonhomme (Stage 2)
Wonderful wild camping over the col des Fours (Stage 3)
(Photos: R.B.Evans)

World Leisure Marketing
Downing Road
West MeadowIndustrial Estate
Derby DE21 6HA

Rand McNally Map Store
10 East 53rd Street
New York
NY
USA

Edward Stanford Ltd
12-14 Long Acre
London WC2E 9LP

Pacific Travellers
529 State Street
Santa Barbara
CA 93101
USA

The Map Shop
15 High Street
Upton upon Severn
Worcs. WR8 0HJ

Waymarks

The basic waymark for the area is a combination of a red and a white stripe, painted horizontally one above the other. More usually this is to be found on wayside rocks but also on posts or the corner of buildings. The three letters TMB take their turn in an occasional substitution for the coloured stripes. Unfortunately their upkeep leaves a little to be desired and in many cases the paint has faded or worn to the point of absence. There are variations in style that will be noted from one valley to another and the Swiss section additionally has clearly displayed signposts, creating a much higher degree of confidence.

Should you encounter the red and white stripes forming a cross, then this is an indication that you have taken a wrong turning, so retrace your steps to sort that out. Too often there is no mark, frequently at a junction where a bit of guidance would not come amiss.

The author is aware that waymarking mainly comes as a result of determined voluntary effort, and it would be foolish to depend purely on the presence of these signs to steer you round the course. Despite the examples of discontinuity in the waymarking, pathfinding is not difficult.

Guided Tours

The most notable operators who offer conducted tours are:

Ramblers Holidays Ltd
Box 43
Welwyn Garden City
Herts. AL8 6PQ
Tel: 01707 331133

Exodus Expeditions
9 Weir Road
London SW12 0LT
Tel: 020 8673 0859

Sherpa
131A Heston Road
Hounslow
Middlesex TW5 0RD
Tel: 020 8577 2717   8/7

No previous experience is demanded other than being generally attuned to fell walking although it is expected that the applicant will undertake to be properly attired and equipped. Operators might stipulate that sleeping bags should be carried to offset the occasional inability to acquire more formal sleeping arrangements. Sherpa have the distinction of having a vehicle which carries provided tenting equipment ahead of the walking group and in consequence it is only necessary to carry a light pack.

Photography

There is probably nothing better than a large format camera to do the Alpine scene justice but weight and space demand equipment of a lighter and more manageable dimension.

35mm-format cameras are the most practical, giving very acceptable results. You can look at the colour pages of most mountaineering magazines and be assured that the majority of these pictures started life in that way. The single lens reflex versions have two advantages over their cousins inasmuch as picture framing is accurate and the by-product of exchangeable lenses is undeniably an asset. A 28mm lens seems to paint a picture, whereas a 100, a 135 or, better still, a 200mm will be useful for closer studies of the peaks or more distant features.

On recent holidays the author has used one of the small 'compacts'. Taking full-frame 35mm film, its results are of the highest order and the fixed 35mm lens produces a pleasing aspect

Astonishing scenery is a feature of the TMB. Here the Aiguille du Géant is seen from above Courmayeur

to the scenery. It has an immaculate self-timer and, being aperture-priority in its operation, allows very accurate lengthy exposure times in dark situations.

Colour reversal (transparency) film gives the best results; they are viewed by projection, although there is a process which will make superb colour prints direct from the transparency. Black and white film is still claimed by some dedicated photographers to give the most feeling and atmosphere, additionally allowing manipulation in the darkroom to modify the effects and the framing. Colour negative has the convenience of readily producing prints of good quality - these are the most convenient for showing to friends and relatives, but quite often it cannot contain the contrast range imposed, resulting in some lack of detail in the brighter areas.

25 or 64 ASA film will usually be found to be quite suitable for the anticipated lighting conditions. The use of a skylight or UV filter is encouraged. Some form of camera support will be invaluable at times, but the use of a full-height tripod is generally ruled out because of its unmanageable shape when it comes to transportation.

Please do not disturb or frighten any animal with your photographic attempts - nor must flowers or plants be damaged.

Additional Information

Tourist Offices in UK

French Government Tourist Office
178 Piccadilly
London W1V 0AL
Tel: 0891 244123

Italian State Tourist Office
1 Princess Street
London W1R 8AY
Tel: 020 7408 1254

Swiss National Tourist Office
Swiss Centre
New Coventry Street
London W1V 8EE
Tel: 020 7734 1921

For the Analytically-Minded

The total distance for the standard Tour works out at around 190km (120 miles). If the complete route has been undertaken then the ascension is equal to the descension at just over 10,000m (33,500ft) and it will be left for you to calculate the intake of liquid fuel (in one form or another) that will be necessary to accomplish it. The excursion to Albert 1er and lac Blanc will add 23km (14 miles) and 1,050m (3,500ft).

Two English walkers known to the author walked from les Houches by the recommended route (every pace!) as far round as the Brévent in four days. Although they did not quite complete the circuit, this represents a very fast time. But so what? Their visual perception of the ground covered must have been of scant consequence. Surely the best measurement should be of what has been seen and not how long it took.

A man from Orsières would currently seem to hold the record for doing the complete Tour. In 1987, at the age of 37 and starting and finishing in Champex, he ran the course in 16hrs 40mins. Good for Lucièn Pellouchoud, but living in the region has given him every opportunity to absorb the scenery at leisure on countless other occasions.

As for going round the TMB circuit in record time, the Swiss relay team that vied with French and Italian teams in 1987 deserve mention. In the highly-organised event known as the *Maratour*, they produced an aggregate timing of 11hrs 54mins to win the event. Once you've been round the TMB yourself you'll marvel at this in disbelief.

By the strangest fluke, the altitude of the *lowest* point passed on the TMB is virtually coincident with the altitude of the *highest* point in England. The bridge over the Arve near to the station at les Houches - the 'Pont des Gures' - has a listed altitude of 980m (3,215ft) compared to Scafell Pike's 977m (3,206ft).

Even the altitude of 1,343m (4,406ft) - the height of Ben Nevis - is encountered at the half-way point on the ascent to the col de Voza which effectively underlines the different scale of things in the TMB region compared to those to which we are accustomed.

Just thought you'd like to know these things.

View towards Bionnassay glacier from path Voza/le Crozat

1: les Houches to les Contamines

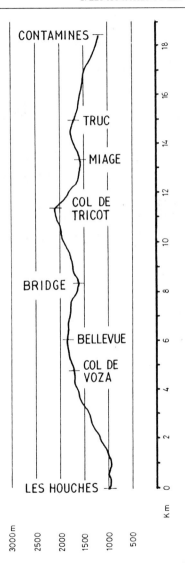

les HOUCHES to les CONTAMINES
8hrs. 18.4km

	Timings: Sectional	Timings: Accumul-ative	Altitude in Metres	Ascent & Descent
les Houches (station)			980	
	0.15	0.15		+31
				-4
les Houches (village)			1007	
	0.15	0.30		+4
				-18
les Houches (Bellevue cableway)			993	
	2.00	2.30		+660
col de Voza			1653	
	0.20	2.50		+133
Bellevue			1786	
	0.45	3.35		+22
				-208
bridge			approx1600	
	1.25	5.00		+520
col de Tricot			2120	
	1.10	6.10		-561
chlts de Miage			1559	
	0.45	6.55		+180
				-19
chlts du Truc			1720	
	1.05	8.00		-553
les Contamines			1167	

totals: +1550
-1363

1: les HOUCHES to les CONTAMINES

As mentioned in the preface, the Tour described in this book assumes a start at les Houches which is at the lower end of the lengthy Chamonix valley.

The author is a strong believer in early departures. It is quite amazing how the hours of the day can slip by, particularly when a succession of attractive views compel frequent halts for photography. At the end of the day it is far better to have more time to relax than to find it becoming a fight to cover that last bit of ground.

Those who are experienced alpine walkers will be in a better position to judge where their landfall will be after their first day on the TMB and getting to Contamines via the col de Tricot for their first night is certainly viable although unaccustomed humidity along with heatwave weather might limit the pace a bit.

However, it is by no means a requirement to reach Contamines at the end of the first day. Truc and Miage are nicely staged to fit in with a more conservative progression and both these places offer overnight accommodation in tranquil locations, well away from the crowds. Staying short of Contamines will give the opportunity of passing through the resort around lunchtime the following day, after which you can saunter up the val Montjoie towards the Nant Borrant premises or those at Balme for your second night.

Arrival by train at **les Houches** will entail a short walk to get to the village. Go down the station approach and over the bridge which spans the river l'Arve. Go up the steep lane that continues from the bridge, turning R to get to the centre of les Houches. Continue walking along the main street until reaching the base station of the les Houches/Bellevue cableway system. The path goes left about fifty paces beyond the station where there is usually a signpost. After 1hr you will approach a T-junction, where turn R. The upper part of the climb is mostly through wooded hillside and hopefully you will have emerged from your climb into the sharp clean air of true Alpine environment, eventually crossing a marshy pasture.

The large building at the col de Voza offers a form of self-service refreshment facility, but the remaining accommodation is private. The author has pitched his tent discreetly on the adjoining hillside on more than one occasion and backpackers could well find a suitable spot there for themselves. The dilapidated building at Bellevue used to offer dortoir accommodation but this was withdrawn when the proprietor went into retirement and, to the knowledge of the author, the facility has yet to be reintroduced - a great pity as the place occupies such a prestigious position and it was a good spot to make for by those coming to the area late in the day and wanting to make a little progress (beverages may still be available). An alternative for those wanting accommodation this soon on the Tour would be to ascend the hillside track that goes up the ridge to the R on reaching the col de Voza to where the Hôtel du Prarion is located.

You will have to bear in mind that practically every stage of the TMB is exposed and once past Voza there is no cover worthy of the description until reaching the final descent into Contamines, notwithstanding the premises at Miage and Truc. So, if the weather is unfavourable, going over the col de Tricot would be inadvisable, in which case it would be safer to go on an alternative route to Contamines. This starts off by descending a broad path to the right once over the railway lines and the col at Voza, passing through the hamlet of Bionnassay (dortoir accommodation), continuing to encounter the valley floor at Bionnay and then trudging up the St. Gervais-Contamines road (possibility of shortening this by taking an obscure path that goes by way of le Chapel on the opposing flank).

It is not all bad news having to go this way: the scenery is still of a high order and it has 'the feel of the mountains' (even if you are at the bottom rather than the top of them) but surely you won't have come all this way just to walk along a road so do press for the high route with all of its scenic advantages unless prudence dictates otherwise.

Getting back on our intended course, the route to the col de Tricot takes an ascending path to the left once over the railway at Voza, climbing bush-covered slopes which level onto a long open ridge known as **Bellevue**. Bellevue, indeed! You will find the commanding 'vue' from here very 'belle' and unless you have previous knowledge of the area, the various peaks will be strangers. To the left, in the near distance, the Brévent summit is clearly discernible, with the Aiguilles Rouges stretching behind, although the eye will understandably be drawn to the bigger range on the right.

The seemingly near-at-hand Dôme du Goûter, 4,304m (14,121ft) dominates the foreground beyond which the rugged Aiguilles du Chamonix hold their stance with the point of Aig. du Midi clearly visible. The Aig. du Midi, 3,842m (12,605ft) has two aids to recognition - not only is there a squat TV/radio transmitting mast secured to its highest point like a stubby finger, but it also houses one of the highest cableway stations in the world at 3,795m and the sharp eye should be able to discern the cabins as they ply their way up and down the steep cable rising from the valley floor. Beyond the Aiguilles, the pleasing shape of Aig. Verte, 4,122m (13,523ft) occupies a position that balances the general aspect. Mont Blanc is the highest of them all at 4,810m (15,781ft) and is the rounded snow-covered summit to the right of the Dôme du Goûter.

At the end of your Tour, in about a fortnight, rest assured that this kind of scenery will have taken on a new and greater significance. Different viewpoints will be discovered as you progress and the names of the significant peaks will become part of everyday conversation. This gradual familiarisation is bound to modify your appreciation of the scenery.

It should be possible to see the glacier des Bionnassay tumbling down from the heights which stem from the higher continuation of the shoulder you are standing on. You will also see the ascending track of the tramway: slightly lower and to its right the eye will be able to trace a footpath and it is this path that must be taken. Initially cutting across the adjacent meadow, it passes through thinly wooded cuttings. Twenty minutes to a dilapidated gate where turn sharp R and downwards (sign: Col de Tricot/Miage). After 7mins L. Another 15mins to reach the rigid wooden bridge that spans the Bionnassay torrent - this is the latest of a succession of bridges and crossings that have come and gone over the years. Another 7mins will bring you to a T-junction, where turn L and up. In 13mins you should have drawn level with a 30-tread galvanised ladder/steps which is intimately close to the snout of the glacier. Massive, isn't it? For the next 7mins the path gets lost as progression is made through the boulder shambles constituting part of the lateral moraine, but be alert to getting R to get back onto the original path, which in another 30mins will deliver you onto a lovely grassy plateau that marks the start of the final climb up to the **col de Tricot**. Backward glances will show the extent of the Bionnassay glacier - of added interest if it is the first one you've ever seen. The path meanders up on the RHS and is well-trod and usually very easy to follow, taking 40mins to reach the col and the stony remains of what was probably a building of some consequence in yesteryear.

Once at the col a different world comes to light: far below you will see the collection of small buildings at **Chlts. de Miage**, and, surprisingly, it will take 1hr 10mins to get down to them. Very often slippery, particularly after rain, you should be cautious of attempting to descend too quickly, even if the thought of food is a driving force! Before you start the descent look at the opposing, but lower, shoulder which represents the location of the Truc chalets - the path leading up to it looks like a zig-zagging thread.

At the dortoir (30 places) and restaurant/bar Chalet de Miage, situated amongst a cluster of premises that are collectively called Chlts. de Miage, it is usual to find comfortable accommodation with substantial food and refreshment. Camping is allowed (ask first). The milk there is of the very best and is available in small quantities in the early evening from a dairy parlour found in one of the stone chalets to the rear of the main building.

The buildings are at the lower end of a 'hanging' valley, the upper end of which has three glaciers suspended from the curved mountain wall. The largest of these is the glacier de Miage and this is the one on the left (the French one, that is, as distinct from the much larger glacier of the same name that falls onto the Italian side of the same ridge and which will be seen in three days' time).

Continue by crossing the bridge and the various waterways concentrated at the place to gain access to the commencement of the path leading up to the Truc shoulder. This is a good and easy path, taking some 45mins. There is a very good refuge (28 places) and restaurant at **Truc**, always a pleasant place for a halt. From outside there is a most commanding view, notably in the general direction of Sallanches which is in the base of the main valley that heads off towards Geneva.

The path now needed continues in the line by which you

arrived, taking only moments to finish crossing the grassy open space and to get onto a rough jeep road between trees. After a short while there is a path dropping to L after the first road zig-zag, and this is very effective in forging a way down until being forced back onto the road.

It will be necessary to stay on this for the remainder of the descent into Contamines whilst inhaling the pine-scented air coming from the thickly-wooded hillside. As you encounter the built-up part of the village, it is possible once more to bisect the winding roadway by following a series of paths which fetch you out at the hub of the village just by the church. Approaching the main junction there's a 'STOP' sign for the motorist but at the end of your first full day you might get the impression that it was really meant for you, being more than grateful for the opportunity to do just that!

Contamines is one of the region's biggest villages. The Tourist Office is centrally placed and exceedingly helpful. Apart from the obvious number of various category hotels, there is a gîte d'étape, a refuge and a campsite which will be found in the locality known as Nivorin, on the other side of the river. The supermarket and other shops seem to open as early as 7.00am, some closing as late as 7.30pm in the evening. Lunchtime closing can be from noon until 3.30pm though. As the subsequent three days are to be spent in desolate country it will be prudent to ensure that the portable larder is adequately stocked. Although meals can usually be obtained en route there are certainly no shops worthy of the name until Courmayeur is reached.

So, what do you think of it all? Probably the average person has some form of discomfort to endure, but after the appropriate attention and a good night's rest the body should be eager to face up to the day that follows.

The cairn at Croix, the refuge lower down and to the right

2: les Contamines to les Chapieux

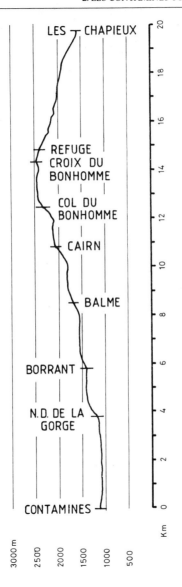

LES CHAPIEUX

REFUGE
CROIX DU
BONHOMME

COL DU
BONHOMME

CAIRN

BALME

BORRANT

N.D. DE LA
GORGE

CONTAMINES

Km

3000 m   2500   2000   1500   1000   500

les CONTAMINES to les CHAPIEUX
6hrs. 40 mins: 19.8km

	Timings		Altitude in Metres	Ascent & Descent
	Sectional	Accumul- ative		
les Contamines			1167	
	0.50	0.50		+49
				−6
N.D. de la Gorge			1210	
	0.40	1.30		+247
Nant Borrant			1457	
	0.50	2.20		+261
				−3
la Balme			1715	
	1.50	4.10		+631
				−17
col du Bonhomme			2329	
	0.40	4.50		+159
				−9
col de la Croix			2479	
	0.10	5.00		−36
ref. de la Croix			2443	
	0.50	5.50		+7
				−444
plan Vararo			2006	
	0.20	6.10		−217
chlts de la Raja			1789	
	0.30	6.40		−235
les Chapieux			1554	
			totals:	+1354
				−967

2: les CONTAMINES to les CHAPIEUX

You are probably getting into the swing of things now and for this particular day an early start is advisable. When you look at the detail of contours, distance and times the route appears quite feasible, but it is simply amazing where the time goes!

Leave **Contamines** by walking south along the main street, beyond the extent of the buildings, until after some 25mins there is a sharp RH turn in the road. At this point, continue straight ahead onto a well-formed path. You will soon discover you have a succession of fast clear running streams for company and attractive tree-clad flanks waft the air with pine scent. In 8mins the path cuts through a large new sports complex. Another 17mins and the luxury of this (almost) level tranquil path comes to an end at **Notre Dame de la Gorge**. The church is quite famous as a tourist landmark and worthy of close inspection, so no doubt the camera will be brought to bear. The adjacent restaurant/bar provides a smoky age-old atmosphere for its patrons.

Retracing the few paces over the bridge brings you to the very base of the steep path which slants up the LH side of the forest-clad ravine. The unusual slabs are generous in their width and provide firm footing for the 30mins that it will take to surmount them. This path is some 2,000 years old. It is believed to be part of the link with the Roman Empire from the heartland of Gaul (the old France). There is usually an enormous board at the bridge indicating the times for the destinations ahead: you might like to study these and compare them firstly with the times detailed in this book and secondly with how long it takes you in the event.

Whilst you climb there is the continual roar of the racing waters to your right. The river in this, the vallée de Montjoie, is called le Bon Nant. At the very head of the slabs, the path levels to cross a very old stone bridge (look over the side and see how years of thrusting water has carved a bizarre chasm some hundred feet below). Ten minutes brings you to the nicely-situated **Hôtellerie de Nant Borrant**. With accommodation for 35 people, mid-day and evening meals are good and substantial. Beverages available continually. Lightweight tenting possible in field below (ask).

The path continues over a stream, up slightly through trees (10mins to where narrower path on L has indication for bivouac camping), then it levels out into open country where the feeling of freshness is quite exhilarating. Towards the end of this flat stretch watch out for a standpipe on LHS (30mins from Borrant) which is a valuable source of water for anyone wanting a cool dowsing just before attempting the steepening path ahead. An extra 20mins brings you adjacent to the **chalets de Balme.**

There are several Balme establishments in the region so don't get confused (particularly with the one referred to later which is situated on the final col as you re-enter the Chamonix valley from Switzerland). This one is particularly pleasant and an ideal spot for lunch. The food has always been to a high standard and is as good a place as any to try your first omelette which are normally extremely appetizing. More substantial mid-day and evening meals are provided. There is sleeping capacity for 56 in their dortoirs with additional turn-of-the-century bedrooms which, for some unknown reason, they seem reluctant to allocate.

Having departed the chalets (2mins: go L onto narrower path), 30mins will be spent climbing to where there is an electricity pylon surmounting a hillock. The view back down the valley is very extensive from here so linger awhile to appreciate it. You have gained substantial altitude and should just about be able to see where Contamines is cradled far below.

The path dips momentarily from the pylon. At the very top of the enormous escarpment confronting you it should be possible to see the orientation table assembly that marks the summit of the Tête Nord des Fours - just to the left of the ridge-mounted pylon carrying the electricity cables (see the final paragraph of this section). After 2mins branch R (usually indicated), and at about 3mins more at a block indicating a National Park you will encounter a fork. R will involve a torrent crossing (can be a problem during or after heavy rain) and L crosses swampy/marshy ground. These two paths eventually merge and pass an enormous **cairn**, 30mins, after climbing a shoulder. This pile of stones is a positive indication that you are not the first traveller in these parts and you are expected to make your own contribution to its growing height.

The path levels and is extremely pleasant, going at half-height along the LH slope of the valley. It turns to R to cross to the other side of the valley which is noticeably narrowing (a trace of late-laying snow, perhaps?). It is then necessary to climb up any one of the many intertwined paths, all of which converge on the col du Bonhomme, 50mins from the cairn. This final part of the climb can be rather irksome but getting into a determined rhythm - however slow - can help enormously. There is a very small shelter at the col which might be of some comfort if there is a cold wind blowing and you want a bit of protection whilst the breath is recovered. Arriving at the **col du Bonhomme** will show the tremendous change in the landscape on the opposing side.

The next port of call is the col de la Croix du Bonhomme. The path begins by walking L (compass bearing 150°) along the saddle that comprises the col du Bonhomme and climbing up about 50ft or so (the small path going off just before the intended one ends at a viewpoint, so take care you have gone high enough). The wanted path veers R and is all but level for what is an extremely relaxing and pleasant walk, and, during its length, there is this new and interesting landscape to survey. You should be feeling rather grand with a sense of relaxed composure, knowing that the main exertions of the day are now well behind! Eventually you will reach a torrent and this is usually crossed by hairpinning up to the L and then coming down to regain the continuing path on the shaly bank opposite, the manoeuvre calling for a little care.

Once past this small problem you should find yourself next to the old marker stone for the **col de la Croix du Bonhomme.** In misty conditions this little corner of the world can be rather tricky. Continue on a level path just to RHS of the marker, curving L slightly and then down centre of a shallow defile until you come to the **refuge du Croix du Bonhomme** (10mins from marker). It can be difficult to find the refuge in poor visibility: it sits at the lower edge of the shallow incline so if you seem to be going very steeply downhill then it is likely that you have passed the place. One way or the other the refuge should be able to accommodate close on 100 people: there is additional space underneath the main building. No spectacular mountains are visible from here although the large conical shape of Mont Pourri, 3,779m (12,398ft), seen directly ahead, is a notable skyline attraction. Staying at high level has certain merits and a night spent here could have its rewards. After nightfall, it would be worth glancing outside just in case moonrise is providing a haunting glow on the surrounding hills. Wakening at Croix, sorting out your gear, washing hurriedly in the freezing water outside and then gulping the gigantic bowl of coffee is guaranteed to put *anyone* into a spartan mood for beginning a day.

As an illustration of how quickly the weather can change, two friends of the author commenced the path from Col du Bonhomme in relatively bright and warm weather. Half-way along it darkened, becoming chilly. Five minutes more and there were flecks of snow. By the time they reached the vicinity of col Croix a blizzard was in progress and the lady of the pair became unwell. It was extremely cold and with the greatest difficulty in the limited visibility they were able to locate the refuge. They and others were trapped there by the snow for three nights, eventually being led down to les Chapieux by a guide. This was in the middle of August.

The best continuation of the walk is to descend to les Chapieux (see alternative later). The path goes off to L in front of the refuge (usually indicated). Shortly sweeping R, it fords many streams as they plummet down their individual ravines. The path begins to cut across more gentle grazing slopes and in 50mins draws level with some cattle buildings where the red/white markings will steer you round their RHS to continue directly behind. The path takes a further 20mins to drop down to a small collection of buildings and a wee stone bridge, chlts. de la Raja. Go along the road that crosses the bridge to seek a path descending from it on L, which keep to for the 30mins it takes to drop to the centre of the charming little hamlet of **les Chapieux.** Charming, but what would it be like without the delightful Hôtel de la Nova? This particular establishment offers a fine table for lunchtime and satisfying evening meals. It has a number of small dortoirs as well as bedrooms and overflow accommodation is taken by two large marquees which have campbeds. There is another hotel in the village, but it seems pretty inactive by comparison, although offering a modest shop facility for the basics.

Alternative route: Coming to les Chapieux has one drawback: on the next day it entails walking for an hour up a tarred road. If one has to walk up a road at all, then there couldn't be a better one (it is described in more detail in the following section) but there is an alternative route to Ville des Glaciers with no roadwork at all.

This involves going over the col des Fours, either by going direct to it from the marker stone at col du Croix or by going up to it from the refuge at Croix (both paths merge after 20mins or so). From the refuge it takes 50mins to get to the col des Fours, where a 25mins + 20mins diversion to the **Tête Nord des Fours** is the 'done thing'. At the Tête there is a *table d'orientation* surmounted by a triangulation of wrought ironwork to mark the spot. It has to be a remarkably clear day to appreciate the true extent of the panorama from the Tête: a list of the prominent places to be seen is lengthy and will certainly include the Matterhorn which is some 80km (50 miles) distant.

As for the col des Fours itself (to which one must return after a detour to the Tête), it is not without its dangers. It has been known for lives to be lost here due to people slipping into a hidden gully during the initial descent. Whilst the Tête represents one of the highest points that could be reached on the Tour (notwithstanding cable-car ascents to Pte. Helbronner and Aig. du Midi later on) the author suggests that there is plenty yet to see that equals or surpasses the impressions obtained at the Tête and so, if you bear with this belief, save the effort involved and go via les Chapieux.

3: les Chapieux to Elisabetta

Aiguille de Trélatête and the Refugio Elisabetta

3: les Chapieux to Elisabetta

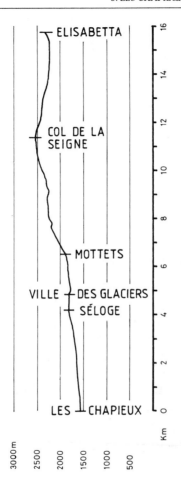

les CHAPIEUX to ELISABETTA
4hrs. 20 mins. 15.6km

	Timings		Altitude in Metres	Ascent & Descent
	Sectional	Accumulative		
les Chapieux			1554	
	0.55	0.55		+226
Seloge			1780	
	0.05	1.00		+9
la Ville des Glaciers			1789	
	0.25	1.25		+119
				−10
les Mottets			1898	
	1.50	3.15		+618
col de la Seigne			2516	
	0.50	4.05		−258
Alpe inf de la Lex Blanche			2258	
	0.15	4.20		+42
Rif. Elisabetta			2300	
			totals:	+1014
				−268

3: les CHAPIEUX to ELISABETTA

The walk over the two cols from Contamines will have done something to toughen up the muscles which will hopefully have relaxed and prepared themselves for another day in the hills. The way out of **les Chapieux** is quite simple: follow the 'high street' for its short length, along which there is an old signpost on the L: 'Mottets/Col de la Seigne/Courmayeur'. Pass the standpipe trough and then up slightly as the narrow road passes a rocky overhang.

Initially it is easy to get the impression that the roadway can hold no joys, but, after only some 15mins the brightly illuminated summit of Aig. des Glaciers shows itself symmetrically in the deep V formed by the narrow and steep-sided part of the vallée des Glaciers up which the road progresses. This delightful spectacle draws the eye for the remainder of the 55mins it takes to get to the chalet at **Séloge**. This quaint little place is situated where the terrain on either side of the road spreads, allowing a better visual impression of the vicinity. As for the premises themselves, well…it is without doubt rather primitive, but the people running the place could not be more attentive and welcoming. The sign outside describes the place as a *Petit Auberge*, offering *fromage de chèvre* (goat's cheese) and a gîte d'étape with dortoir facilities.

The roadway surface deteriorates in the 5mins or so taken to get to the cluster of sheds known as **Ville des Glaciers**. With a name like this one could be forgiven for expecting not only an active village but uncountable glaciers. As it happens, there is only one dominant glacier - the glacier des Glaciers - and, as for a village, well…no. The best on offer here is the standpipe and you are recommended to fill up the bottles as there is no guarantee of another opportunity until you reach the Elisabetta refuge.

It is here that those who crossed the col des Fours make their appearance, having descended from there in some 1hr 50mins. Turn R and in less than 2mins you will be crossing the bridge over the greyish waters of the river called Torrent des Glaciers. At least the waters are here to be seen: on the way up from les Chapieux you will have noticed the dam (the French call it a *barrage*) that is all part of their hydro-electric network and it is these catchments that are denying the lower valleys of their water flow. Be careful if contemplating a dip in this river because, as with other glacier-fed torrents, the greyish appearance is caused by the suspension of minuscular grit which has much the same effect as taking a bath with 'scouring powder' in it!

Once over the bridge the well-formed path veers left. A sign states that camping is not permitted from this point up as far as the col because it is private land; although the validity of this would be tiresome to check. People have certainly been known to erect their tents in the vicinity of the **Mottets** refuge, albeit with permission from the guardian. Another sign says: 'Courage - des Mottets in 15mins!' This mythical '15mins' will take every bit of 30 and, because the buildings are hidden until the last moment, helps create the impression that it has been missed. It takes 25mins to reach a junction where the spur path on the L takes an additional 5mins to get to this refuge. Due to its large outbuildings, accommodation is probably in the order of 80 places. Food is limited in choice, but the wine is notably cheap.

There is a newish gîte d'étape situated as far upstream as the Mottets but on the other side of the river. Those who have stayed there speak highly of the place and the overall impression is that it is a converted chalet and more snug than the larger place. Access to it would be by continuing straight ahead when passing through the Ville des Glaciers instead of crossing the bridge. Should you visit this lodging place, then it is not necessary to go back to the Ville to rejoin the path. A hairpinning descending path from the place finds a bridge to cross the torrent and a continuing path comes up past the Mottets premises where it takes the same 5mins to get to the path junction referred to earlier.

From the junction, the path sweeps up over the relatively flat grassy ground until encountering the steep hillside where the inevitable hairpin path aids the ascent. Taken at an even pace progress becomes noticeable and soon you will be able to look down on the Mottets buildings as they seemingly diminish in size - the large white painted MOTTETS lettering on the roof obviously being intended as an advertisement for walkers coming in the other direction. Shortly, the path dips to cross a ravine where the water flow can be quite strong but there should be enough large rocks protruding to act as stepping stones. From here the path cants L to

The head of the vallée des Glaciers with the Aiguille des Glaciers.
The TMB climbs up to the right to cross the col de la Seigne

mount the final hillside. The glacier on the L is the eyecatcher but disappears from sight as the path becomes a broad scar and straightens to the R, eventually reaching its highest point on the shoulder of the **col de la Seigne** - the Franco/Italo border, 1hr 50mins from the Mottets path junction.

The final approach to the col is relatively level and along this part of the walk you should be aware of an increasing vista beginning to rise just to the L beyond the col which, in clear weather, should have an exhilarating effect and counteract any feeling of fatigue. Mont Blanc can be seen from the col but the nearest feature is of the whitish-green peaks in the near foreground, known as Pyramides Calcaires. The view straight ahead is almost as mind boggling as it is unexpected. You can see not only the length of val Vény, but continuing along through the (Italian) val Ferret to the col Grand Ferret, the scene of your next prominent exploit. Half-way along all this, on the RH hillside, you should be able to discern the conical shape of Mont Chétif, marking the upper end of the beautiful val d'Aosta, behind which the resort of Courmayeur is located. Slightly nearer, the grey scar coming down into the valley from the L is the RH lateral moraine of the glacier du Miage which will be passed at close quarters after the Elisabetta Hut.

Having arrived at the col de la Seigne 'head on', there is a tendency to go straight over and down the centre of the bowl on the Italian side and some maps show this as being the way. Often this bowl has late-lying snow, and the traces of footprints down its centre continue to attract people that way. Actually, you should turn R (compass bearing: 165°) and walk some 200 paces along the saddle: this will pass the rocky seam on the R immediately dropping to where there is a small but derelict stone building, where, turning L, you will encounter the upper part of the descending path. The path is substantial and, after swinging to the L to reach the floor of a terraced valley, it veers R after crossing a stream to take a total of 50mins to draw level with a few old barns at Alp inf. de la Lex Blanche.

Turn sharp L and climb for 10mins to reach the **Elisabetta refuge.** This refuge was completed as a memorial to Italian Alpine troops and is well equipped for the tourist. There is a resident chef and the food is generally plentiful, albeit with an understandable leaning to the Italian dishes. There are three styles of accommodation - providing your arrival is early enough to allow selection: individual rooms for two, rooms for a dozen or so and the traditional dormitory. The refuge will hold something like 90 people but can double that on a stormy night when additional people seek shelter there and it becomes necessary to sleep on the corridor floors. Toilet door labelling takes some understanding in Italy, and the refuge will be the first encounter with the problem: *Signore* or *Donne* = Ladies, *Uomini* or *Signori* = Men.

The refuge is proudly situated in a prestigious position overlooking the snout of the glacier de la Lex Blanche and facing lac Combal, where the dominant feature of the main mountain range is the over-bearing shape of the Aig. Noire de Peutery 3,772m (12,375ft). Lac Combal is the name given to the rivulet-strewn area that occupies the expanse below the refuge and through which the path described in the next section makes further progress in the direction of Courmayeur.

Right: The peaks of the Mont Blanc range reflected in
Chécrouit Lake above val Veni

4: Elisabetta to Courmayeur

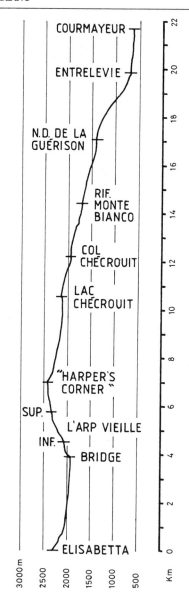

ELISABETTA to COURMAYEUR
5hrs. 15 mins. 21.7km

	Timings		Altitude in Metres	Ascent & Descent
	Sectional	Accumul-ative		
Rif. Elisabetta			2300	
	0.10	0.10		− 42
Alpe inf de la Lex Blanche			2258	
	0.50	1.00		− 288
lac Combal, bridge			1970	
	0.18	1.18		+ 103
l'Arp Vieille inf			2073	
	0.37	1.55		+ 230
l'Arp Vieille sup			2303	
	0.20	2.15		+ 137
Harper's corner			2440	
	1.05	3.20		+ 16
				− 291
lac Chécrouit			2165	
	0.20	3.40		− 209
col Chécrouit			1956	
	0.25	4.05		− 256
rif Monte Bianco			1700	
	0.25	4.30		− 195
road junction			1505	
	0.05	4.35		− 61
N.D. de la Guérison			1444	
	0.25	5.00		− 218
bridge, Entrelevie			1226	
	0.15	5.15		+ 6
				− 12
Courmayeur			1220	
			totals:	+ 492
				− 1572

4: ELISABETTA to COURMAYEUR

It is not obligatory to stay at the **Elisabetta refuge**; competent walkers probably finding that they arrive quite early. But those who have not got a tent would have to find shelter and the next places are a long way further on (col Chécrouit, by the recommended 'high route': 3hrs 45mins and the Cantine de la Visaille, by the 'valley floor route': 2hrs 15mins).

* * *

No alarm clock will be needed at Elisabetta as the voices of many nationalities along with the general clatter will get you awake and heading for the washroom. Soon after fighting for your share of the coffee pot, you will be out in the mountain air once again.

Drop from the refuge for 10mins to rejoin the main path at the cattle sheds. This then descends the shoulder separating the two terraces, where the hairpinning stony roadway can be avoided by taking the overgrown path, eventually levelling at the makeshift car park space level with lac Combal. From there it is necessary to walk along the causeway road where the enormity of the Miage glacier's lateral moraine sweeps down from L to R. At the end of the lake the road turns L to cross a stone bridge and it is to here that buses come throughout the day from Courmayeur. If you go over the bridge and turn L there is a bar, obviously a focal point worth knowing about, 5mins. A series of short paths above the bar lead up to lac du Miage which has the unusual feature of sometimes having blocks of ice floating in it that have separated from the rock-covered glacier which takes a definite LH turn at this point. It does not pretend to be Italy's answer to Greenland's vast iceberg spawning coastline but many find it attractive.

Getting back to the route proper, there are two ways of reaching Courmayeur. One is down the valley floor, virtually continuing on the road that descends past the moraine wall through the Cantine de la Visaille. Beyond this place the valley floor widens becoming pastoral and graceful. But only go by this route if there is extremely bad weather or a low cloud base as the better way to go is by the high route which starts just before the bridge at the point where it was

At the col de la Seigne. View towards val Vény and the Italian side of Mont Blanc (Stage 3)   (Photo: A.Harper)

The Elisabetta refuge lies below the Lex Blanche glacier (Photo: R.B.Evans)

initially approached. Slanting up to the right (its steepness is not prolonged), it takes 18mins to get to the cluster of dilapidated shacks that bear the name of **l'Arp Vieille Inferior** and then 37mins to get to the cattle sheds at **l'Arp Vieille Superior**. Between these two places the height gained permits backward glances over to lac du Miage and you will be able to see if it has any floes.

Forging ahead, the path curves to L and zig-zags a little to get higher up the shoulder, eventually reaching an obvious high point in an additional 22mins. Someone suggested that this nameless spot ought to be christened 'Harper's Corner', but imagine what the Italians might think of that idea! The path continues by dropping sharply, then settles at an almost horizontal level for the 1hr 5mins it will take to get to the once-lovely setting of **lac Chécrouit**. The lake itself hasn't changed much over the years, but it is impossible to ignore the surrounding desecration created by the lust for even more ski-runs. The lake is often depleted of water late in the season, but when it is full it is the aim of most photographers to use it for mirror-imaging their shot of the Italian face of Mont Blanc which is at this point directly opposite.

Let's turn for a while to the scenery opposing us across the val Vény. Its presence cannot have escaped you whilst you have been walking from 'Harper's Corner'. Even in mist the fleeting cloud will provide tempting sightings, but in clear weather the whole thing can be an indescribable joy. The magnitude of it all is staggering and this superb balcony walk offers continual and magnificent visual impressions. The rocky and icy amphitheatre is worthy of ceaseless study and so you must take it all in as best you can. If it can be improved on at all, then it can only be from the crest of Monte de la Saxe - a walk which is described later.

Over the last few years the continuation of the path beyond lac Chécrouit has been a shambles. The bulldozed slopes have obviously ruined the original path and there has been a futile attempt at its restoration. Proceed as best as possible in an almost level line beyond the position of the lake then dropping slightly, keeping close to the RH fence and bushes (if these are still there: further alterations are not to be ruled out). Twenty minutes of this will bring you to a small defile and into the clearing marking the position of **col**

Chécrouit where there is the relatively new refuge, the Maison Vieille, which has dortoir capacity for 50 people and an associated restaurant/bar. The premises are ideally situated, facing directly down the upper confines of the Aosta valley with the foothills of the enormous Gran Paradiso range dominant on the R. A fine sight.

The way from here used to continue ahead to plan Chécrouit but this has become treacherous and difficult, so marking the end of any desire to continue recommending it as the way down. Fortunately the alternative path has attractions of its own and to get onto this turn sharp L at the refuge, crossing the small grassy plateau behind, where at the trees an idyllic little path threads its way down the hillside. After some 12mins it reaches a clearing accommodating a ski-lift terminal: forge down the immediate bank and then turn sharp R onto a gritty wide slope which runs down to the **rif. Monte Bianco**, 13mins. More like a hotel than a refuge, it also appears to cater for motorists and has an active trade. From the vicinity of the refuge there are splendid views to be had of the val Vény as well as the ramparts of the Aig. Noire de Peuterey which are met head-on and at close quarters.

Unfortunately from this point down it is necessary to walk along the roadside but there's no need to grumble because, as road walks go, it couldn't be much nicer. Straight ahead and high up you will see the dominant shape of the Grandes Jorasses, 4,208m (13,806ft), with its white-capped summit and to its L the characteristic stub of the Dent du Géant (Giant's tooth), 4,014m (13,169ft). Lower down you can discern Mont Frétey which is where the ascending cableway from la Palud to Helbronner has its intermediate station. After 25mins bear R where this minor road forks into the main valley road that comes down from Cantine de la Visaille. Over on the left is the enormity of the boulder-strewn tongue of the Brenva glacier: at first sight it looks like a horrendous heap of rocks, but ice can be seen protruding here and there.

The rivers coming from the two valleys (la Doire de Vény and la Doire de Ferret) converge to become the Doire Baltée. The aim is to cross this torrent as it turns down into the head of the val d'Aosta so that you can cross to the opposite bank for continuing the walk up the flanks of the val Ferret. It takes 30mins down the road to get to the first bridge, but the views to the L become open and some of this time can be spent by observing the activities surrounding the entrance to the Mont Blanc road tunnel. You will pass the unusual and charming **Notre Dame de la Guérison** but don't get too wound up with photographic enthusiasm unless you have a 13mm lens in the outfit! This little chapel is perched precariously on the RH mountainside and is not without its obligatory novelty shop in attendance.

Having reached the bridge at **Entrelevie** and crossed, turn R along a minor road which in some 15mins will bring you to the top end of the mountaineering resort of Courmayeur with its obvious selection of hotels, restaurants, shops and facilities. **Courmayeur** is a busy place and if you want somewhere a little more tranquil to stay then recommendation must favour Entrèves which is a charming little mountain village that has not lost its character even though it has to withstand the effects of a major highway curving round its perimeter. It, too, has numerous places to stay along with several restaurants and bars and you could expect to get a more favourable deal by staying here rather than in Courmayeur.

To reach **Entrèves** turn L at the bridge from where it will take 25mins to get to the centre of the village. In Appendix 1 (Time in Courmayeur) one of the suggestions is to take a cable-car up to Pte. Helbronner and if this is your intention then staying two nights in Entrèves will prove ideal, as the base station at la Palud is only a few minutes away. There is dortoir accommodation available at the Albergo Funivia in la Palud. On the other hand you could always go up to the Torino refuge and sleep the night there, but to achieve this it would be necessary to reach la Palud before the last cable-car has departed - about 5.30pm. The rif. Torino generally offers full evening dinner as well as bar service to create the usual comforts. After witnessing a most spectacular sunrise, you could have breakfast up there too and be down in the valley by 10.00am ready to put muscle into continuing the TMB. Up to you!

Mont Blanc from la Vachey

5: Courmayeur to la Vachey

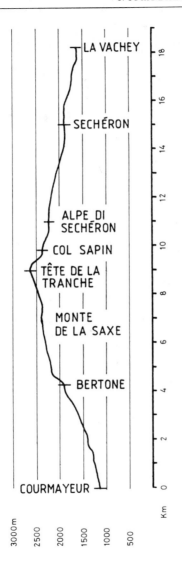

LA VACHEY

SECHÉRON

ALPE DI
SECHÉRON

COL SAPIN

TÊTE DE LA
TRANCHE

MONTE
DE LA SAXE

BERTONE

COURMAYEUR

3000m 2500 2000 1500 1000 500

Km

COURMAYEUR to la VACHEY
by way of Monte de la Saxe and col Sapin
4hrs. 50mins. 18km

	Timings		Altitude in Metres	Ascent & Descent
	Sectional	Accumulative		
Courmayeur			1220	
	0.15	0.15		+107
Villair			1327	
	1.20	1.35		+664
la Pré, rif. Bertone			1991	
	0.12	1.47		+134
Monte de la Saxe (start)			2125	
	0.23	2.10		+223
(highest point on ridge)			2348	
	1.00	3.10		+222
adj Tête de la Tronche			2570	
	0.10	3.20		−134
col Sapin			2436	
	0.20	3.40		−161
Alpe de Séchéron			2275	
	0.40	4.20		−351
Séchéron			1924	
	0.30	4.50		−282
la Vachey			1642	
			totals:	+1350
				−928

COURMAYEUR to la VACHEY
by way of Entrèves and the valley floor
2hrs. 45mins. 10.5km

	Timings		Altitude in Metres	Ascent & Descent
	Sectional	Accumulative		
Courmayeur			1220	
	0.15	0.15		+ 12
				− 6
Entrelevie			1226	
	0.25	0.40		+ 80
Entrèves			1306	
	0.10	0.50		+ 64
la Palud			1370	
	0.40	1.30		+ 228
Planpincieux			1598	
	0.35	2.05		+ 26
				− 4
Tronchey			1620	
	0.40	2.45		+ 22
la Vachey			1642	
			totals:	+ 432
				− 10

5: COURMAYEUR to la VACHEY

Pray for good weather as the visual prospects for the route about to be described are spectacular, and, inevitably, it needs conditions of clarity. It should also be free of snow or it becomes precarious in its later stages. The walk starts plumb in the middle of **Courmayeur**, heading up the narrow street adjacent to the church from where it takes some 15mins to pass through the length of **Villair**. At the upper end of this village, continue straight onto what will have become an unmade road, through trees and then to the bridge with its man-made waterfalls splaying the water coming down under it, 10mins. Cross the bridge where the road veers to L and at its first hairpin you should take the path going up on L which bisects the sweeping zig-zags of the road. In 11mins you will be forced onto the road again and then, some 50 paces along road to R, you should see another path on L signposted: 'le pré de la Saxe/rifugio Bertone - path 25'.

This is a lovely path, sometimes open and then slightly shaded, and is excellent almost the whole way up to this relatively new refuge called **Bertone**, 1hr 8mins. At 38mins there is an enormous rock that has obviously been manipulated to act as a bench seat, where someone has painted an encouraging '2/3', but with only 1/3 to go you might not want to break your pace!

Bertone is idyllically positioned just above the treeline, set on a promontory that faces Mont Chétif across the neck of the val d'Aosta. From the terrace it is possible to look down onto the miniaturised buildings of Courmayeur, the church you left just two hours ago clearly distinguishable. If the church can be seen from here, then surely the refuge can be seen from the church? One is struck by the general absence of birdlife in the Mont Blanc region nowadays but the wooded hills leading up to Bertone seem to have more than their fair share. Bird song is a constant accompaniment to the walk up and butterflies were well in evidence during the author's last visit.

Bertone has 54 dortoir-style places, and offers meals at mid-day and in the evening with what appears to be a continual bar and snack service. Relaxing there in strident sunshine will compensate for any previous foul weather. But don't sit for too long as there is still quite a way to go and you are bound to find the progress a stop/go affair due to the scenery.

Leave the refuge by going up diagonally R to pass a shepherd's (?) chalet. Then more directly up the hillside, where a path coming up from the other side meets at a panorama table. Go R here, surmounting the final slopes by the worn paths. Even at the panorama table, you begin to sense the glories of the view. You should be able to see right along the floor of val Vény, past the split tongue of the Miage glacier, the Pyramides Calcaires, to the col de la Seigne. But, oh, the glory of Mont Blanc with its vast abutments, all of which are individually named and famous in their own right. The eye is tormented, not knowing where to look, as it is all too magnificent for words. It takes 35mins to get right to the top of the crest of **Monte de la Saxe** and then more comes to view. The notable attraction then becomes the Grandes Jorasses and the whole range gels into one supreme visual balance.

Walking along the crest of Monte de la Saxe in dazzling sunshine can be a highly rewarding experience and only an insensitive person would be unaffected by its loveliness. At the far end of the hump the path dips and this seems to be where the accompanying 'path 25' waymarks cease, 15mins. At this point a path goes off L to get to the val Ferret in a more direct manner than the way about to be described, but practically everyone finds difficulty with this lower down and there have been regular tales of woe. Instead of dipping down, maintain altitude by selecting the track which leads in the general direction of the Tête Bernard, the rock-sided summit that confronts you (compass bearing 70°). Five minutes to pass through a shallow defile, then in 12mins four or five little hillocks mark the end of Monte de la Saxe, where there is a handsome dew pond that will allow that 'reflection' photograph.

Then climb gently (bearing 75°) going slightly R of **Tête Bernard** and cross a narrow band of scree/rock, that is 'in line' with the summit, 13mins. Sweeping R slowly and contouring in 12mins you will come to the first notch in what has now become a steep cliff falling away on the L. The notch provides a commanding view over the valley down which you will stroll in an hour's time after having gained access to it by the col de Sapin, but **don't** attempt to descend into it from here! Continue by keeping on the faint path going parallel to the cliff edge (bearing 120°) and in another 8mins you will encounter the rocky approaches to **Tête de la Tronche**, the highest of the two peaks.

The path veers to the L to avoid clambering over the summit and then turns R to begin the expected descent, taking only 8mins to drop to the col by a fairly steep but safe path. Compass bearings are quoted because of the lack of waymarks on this tetchy final stretch and to comfort the walker who might encounter misty conditions. Cautionary mention must be made of the obvious increase in difficulty that late snow or ice would impose on the final 20mins or so of this approach to col Sapin. One would then be advised to retreat to the vicinity of the dew pond and drop down to val Ferret as best as one can: it might be clumsy, but at least it would be relatively safe.

Col Sapin sits amidst a broad saddle and coming up to it from the right is a more direct path from Courmayeur. Note that the upper stretches of this particular path are steep and irksome and lack the visual attractions of the Monte de la Saxe route: this is because Monte de la Saxe itself intervenes and prohibits extensive views until late in the ascent.

Having come to the col it is necessary to turn L, where a series of easy paths eventually cross a small torrent, 20mins where turn L again to go down the centre of the valley just on the immediate right of the stream. You are not advised to go quite as far as the cowsheds at **Alpe de Séchéron**. This is because the path continuing from there is overgrown and badly maintained at several earthslips and stone chutes. Whilst concentrating on the walk towards the Tête de la Tronche you had to turn your back on the massive bulk of the Gds. Jorasses, but here it is again: framed directly ahead - what a showstopper for the end of the day!

The path swings R round the end of this hanging valley, permitting an almost vertical view down to the base of val Ferret in the vicinity of la Vachey. From Alpe de Séchéron it takes 40mins to draw level with the deserted cowsheds at the lower **Séchéron** and then a further 20mins to drop down to encounter the valley road at a spot which is further up the valley than la Vachey. If you wanted to go straight towards col Gd. Ferret then you would turn R, but, for la Vachey, turn L, walk along the road and just before its first

The Italian val Ferret with the Grandes Jorasses

descending hairpin watch out for paths on RHS which makes quick work of the easy descent.

La Vachey boasts two hotels, only the Hôtel la Vachey offering accommodation. Both establishments provide evening meals but after a hot day in the hills it is probably only the bar service that will be the immediate attraction! Despite common belief, lightweight camping is feasible by going to the pasture on the far (ie. NNW) side of the valley opposing the hotels, attained by crossing the main road bridge in front of the hotels and then a subsidiary bridge to R (might be advisable to ask at Hôtel Dolent first).

THE VALLEY FLOOR ROUTE

In really poor visibility or if the snowline is low down it would obviously be a waste of effort to attempt the route just described. The route up the valley floor is not without merit and the author has never tired of the stroll, although some others regard it as a bit of a plod. Effectively it starts at **la Palud**, following the roadway where most of the bends can be short cut by paths. Watch for an unmade stony road slanting off to R (just after a path leads down to a bridge

71

marked Pont Atellier) which will take you off the main road for 20mins to bring you into **Planpincieux** with its few hotels, restaurants and bars. Further along the road is the enormous Grandes Jorasses camping site which could be of service, then the wee chapel which is just before le Pont and Tronchey. **Tronchey** would seem to offer some form of dortoir facility so maybe that is worthy of an on-the-spot investigation. The road curves in a sweep to the L before finally turning to the R and crossing the bridge to reach the location of la Vachey hotels. The valley buzzes with a hive of pursuits that include golfing, pony-trekking, cycling on hired bikes, tennis, trout fishing, jogging and so on, and watching all this activity is quite absorbing.

The setting of **la Vachey** is as nice as one would wish. Tranquillity is only broken by the occasional reversing car and the squeal of the bus brakes every hour or so. The waters in the adjacent stream are crystal clear, making the polished stones on the bed look brighter than if they were held in the hand. The aspects of the valleysides are daunting, particularly those forming the sheer base of the unseen Jorasses. At dusk, the silhouette of Mont Blanc supported by the Peuterey makes fascinating study and, to quote the author's son: '...this is a sight I will always remember!'

Before going into the text of Stage 6, perhaps mention ought to be made of the existence of the nicely-appointed **Elena** refuge which is situated at the upper end of the Italian val Ferret.

The original Elena was destroyed by avalanche about 1961 and its replacement was inaugurated in 1992. Its facility was sadly missed during the intervening years mainly because its position offers the possibility of a much more economic progression at this corner of the TMB. Prior to its reconstruction the overnights were restricted to la Vachey with nothing available after that until Ferret which is well over on the Swiss side of the col separating the two places.

The Elena is probably too far to contemplate for those leaving Courmayeur and progressing the Monte de la Saxe variant but by the time you reach the environs of Courmayeur you will be in as good a position as anyone to assess your performance for what lies ahead. Staying at the Bertone refuge would give a better assurance of getting to the Elena that same evening, as certainly as going up

72

the valley floor past la Palud and Planpincieux, both of which should present no difficulties timewise. For those who want to avail themselves of mechanical aids along the way, note that there is a regular bus service from Courmayeur going as far as the premises at Arnuva.

Residing at Elena would create the possibility of reaching Champex, say, for the ensuing night whereas the practicality of getting that far from la Vachey has proved a couple of km too far for the author (and others he has met!) on the two occasions he has attempted it.

The Pré de Bar glacier seen from the path to the Col du Grand Ferret

6: la Vachey to la Fouly

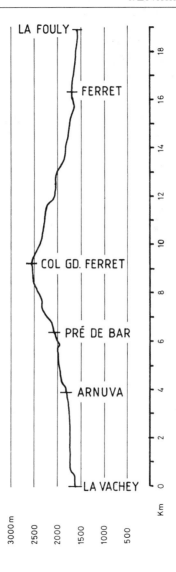

LA FOULY

FERRET

COL GD. FERRET

PRÉ DE BAR

ARNUVA

LA VACHEY

Km

3000 m 2500 2000 1500 1000 500

La VACHEY to la FOULY
5hrs. 05mins. 18.4km

	Timings		Altitude in Metres	Ascent & Descent
	Sectional	Accumul-ative		
La Vachey			1642	
	0.50	0.50		+127
Arnuva			1769	
	0.45	1.35		+293
Pré de Bar/Elena			2062	
	1.20	2.55		+475
Gd. col Ferret			2537	
	0.50	3.45		−466
la Peule (troughs)			2071	
	0.25	4.10		−296
bridge			1775	+8
	0.25	4.35		−83
Ferret			1700	
	0.30	5.05		−105
la Fouly			1595	
			totals:	+903
				−950

6: La VACHEY to la FOULY

This will not represent a full day to the competent walker although it is not without its energies. Referring to the footnote of the last section, the re-introduction of the Elena offers a more efficient staging: ELENA to PRAZ de FORT for instance. As the Elena was not in existence for so many years, its position on some maps might not be marked. It is actually situated on a small shelf named Alpe superior de Pré de Bar at altitude 2,202m where it has been built into the cliff face at the forward edge of this small plateau, undoubtedly as a safeguard against further avalanche threats.

* * *

Initially, take the road that passes the frontage of the hotels at **la Vachey** for the 5mins or so that it takes to reach the spot where the road starts to climb. In a direct line opposite you should be able to see the track that short cuts the road hairpins and in 10mins the roadway is rejoined where it levels. The road is in a clump of trees at this section, where you will see the path going off R to Séchéron and col Sapin. Continue along the road and as it emerges from the trees you cannot but fail to notice how savage the valley floor has become, particularly lower to the L where the evidence of raging melt waters during the early-summer thaw is only too obvious.

It is extremely pleasant strolling along this quiet road first thing in the morning. The air is usually rare and chill, and the visibility can be without bounds. Drawing level with the **Arnuva** chalets (possible accommodation) will have clocked up 50mins from la Vachey and now the walk *really* begins. This is currently as far as cars can progress up the valley, and a few paces beyond is an area set aside as a car park, RHS.

There is an obvious continuing track, wide enough to take farm vehicles, and you head along this for only a few paces where you should see a signpost on R. Go up this path which soon surmounts a grassy shoulder, zig-zags a couple of times and then heads in the general direction that is parallel to the track you have just abandoned and in 20mins you draw level with a derelict stone building. A further 25mins on a continuing path contours round the hillside, dipping to ford a tumbling stream, and then up to the site of the original Elena refuge where the granite blocks of its foundations are still evident.

The backward view from here oversees not only the valley it is in but val Vény beyond. You should be able to make out the paths crossing Chécrouit, just beyond Chétif (Chétif looks small from here), then in the far distance, the col de la Seigne with the Pyramides Calcaires to its R. You might discern what is known as 'le Jardin' that bisects the snout of the mighty Miage glacier.

Continue by going past the RHS of the old refuge and in 5mins you will find yourself on the small plateau known as **Pré de Bar** where there is usually a water pipe at the trough in front of the cattle sheds. Bivouac camping is frequent at this magnificent spot, but there should be no need for that now that the new refuge here is available for your custom. At the far end of this grassy plateau the traditional path will be seen to come up from the L (it is a most uninteresting path, taking some 20mins longer than the attractive alternative just described). At this exact spot there is the most wonderful view of the Pré de Bar glacier. You will be able to marvel at the way it has squeezed through the rocky defile that has attempted to restrain it, fanning out symmetrically before petering away to contribute melt water for the valley streams. The high moraine walls - long since deserted by the retracting ice - are a precise indication of how this glacier has diminished in recent times.

The upward path continues at the higher end of this plateau on an obvious diagonal well-trodden scar until a series of zig-zags reach a derelict stone building, 32mins. Go up the path behind the ruins for a little further where there is a signpost, at which point you must turn sharp L and ascend a little more before getting to the final approaches which become exposed and level out to give commanding views towards the Gds. Jorasses and the mountain walls behind the Pré de Bar glacier. Following a broad sweep along a cliff edge, the **col du Grand Ferret** comes into sight and 10mins later you get your first clear view from it of Switzerland. The snow-capped mountain in the distance is the Grand Combin, 4,090m (13,418ft). To the left, following the line of the saddle, you will see Mont Dolent, 3,823m (12,542ft), the summit of which is shared by

78

France, Switzerland and Italy as this is where their frontiers meet. At the col there is a *table d'orientation* with a line heading off to the east labelled 'Matterhorn' but it might just as well say 'Bombay' because *neither* can be seen from there.

Another interesting thing to consider about the col is that it, like the col de la Seigne, is a watershed for different rivers. A drop of rain falling on the Italian side of both these cols will help to make up the flow of the Doire Baltée and, once in the plain between Turin and Milan and along with other tributaries, becomes the Po which reaches the Adriatic Sea just south of Venice. Water from the other side of these cols will become part of the Rhône. The water getting past les Chapieux flows to Bourg St. Maurice to swell the Isère, then through Grenoble to join the main flow of the Rhône at Valence. The water falling on the Swiss side of the col Ferret will have flowed into the Drance to pass Orsières and to join the Valais section of the Rhône at Martigny which then flows into lake Geneva near Montreux. The water from the Contamines and Chamonix area flows as the Arve to link with the younger Rhône at Geneva that has issued from lake Geneva. The Rhône eventually flows into the Mediterranean near Marseilles.

The terrain is noticeably different on the other side of the pass; gentle banks of grass and much more passive. The path dips from the col then strikes off L to round a hollow. If it should be under snow, staves usually mark the way. After 8mins fork L to go up and centrally cross a dip formed in the LH mountainside, taking a further 2mins. Providing you have gone far enough across, there is the most far-reaching and stupendous view to be had right down the (Swiss) val Ferret to its furthest extent and perhaps you can see the dot-sized buildings that represent the resort of Verbier, itself high on the hillsides above Orsières. The narrow light-grey triangle of bare rock slanting down L to R marks the approximate position of Champex, although a belvedere hotel might also be visible which would pinpoint the place precisely. The mountains way yonder are part of the Oberland group.

Regain the original path and follow its gentle sweep downwards. The main wall faced over the valley you are approaching divides val Ferret from val d'Entremont, down which the main highway from col du Gd. St. Bernard links Aosta and Martigny.

In 42mins you will be at a small plateau. Cattle are kept at this height and there is an enormous 5-tub trough placed for their thirsts. On extremely hot days people have been known to immerse themselves full-clothed in an attempt to get cool but they ignored the *'défence de salir l'eau'* sign. They should have been advised to wait the additional 25mins it takes to reach the valley. Cross over the field, start descending the jeep road until encountering the head of a series of paths which drop right down to a bridge, where the fast-flowing cold water is capable of even greater service than the trough.

The view from the bridge is delightful, with the river's pine-clad banks balancing the mighty mountainous scenery beyond. At the end of the summer the banks of the river are carpeted with tall mauve-budded plants which are also to be seen in vast quantities on other parts of the route. They are called *épilobes*.

There is a sign near the bridge, positioned for the benefit of the backpacker entering the val Ferret from Italy, which makes it quite clear that camping in the whole of the Swiss val Ferret is prohibited other than at the two official sites at la Fouly and Champex. The la Fouly campsite, Camping du Glacier, is vast and attractively positioned whereas the Champex site, Camping des Rocailes, is fairly compact, if not exactly cramped, although both are nicely staged. The bridge is coincident with the head of the roadway plying the valley, although it doesn't seem to have a lot of traffic. **Ferret** is the first village some 25mins down the road where there is a large hotel and a dortoir/restaurant.

The restaurant facilities at the latter establishment, the Restaurant du col Fenêtre, are particularly rewarding after an energetic morning but it is essential to arrive by 1.30pm in order to be assured of lunch service. On a nice day, there is probably nothing finer than sitting under a sunshade on their immaculately-kept grass terrace and imbibing to taste, knowing that it's all downhill in the afternoon, and a short afternoon at that!

Maps show a short path going down from these premises to cross the river and then turning R to go along the valley floor to get to la Fouly, but it doesn't seem worth the taking. Note the pleasant little *chapelle de Ferret* at la Ferret (photographers note - a 25mm lens is the tool for the job here) and then set off down the side of the road

80

where it takes exactly half an hour to walk into the centre of **la Fouly**. This is quite a large village and amongst others, the hôtel Edelweiss has an additional attraction inasmuch as it has a nice dortoir in the attic area. Mention has already been made of the campsite. As you were about to enter the village you probably noticed a path leaving the road on L, cutting down to a bridge. Access to the campsite is made by crossing this bridge, turning first R and continuing over another bridge and *voila!* - the campsite. The heart of the village has shopping facilities to meet your current needs as well as a PTT (Post Office). There is a Tourist Office which is situated on the slip road leading down to the bridge. Buses come this far from Orsières, the railhead town linking with Martigny.

In the Swiss val Ferret

7: la Fouly to Champex/Arpette

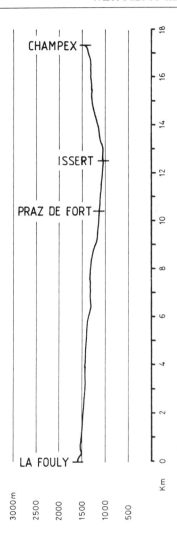

la FOULY to CHAMPEX
by the normal route
4hrs. 25mins. 17.3km

	Timings		Altitude in Metres	Ascent & Descent
	Sectional	Accumulative		
la Fouly			1595	
	0.15	0.15		+ 14
				− 17
campsite			1592	
	0.30	0.45		− 112
adj Prayon			1480	
	0.50	1.35		− 90
adj Branche			1390	
	0.40	2.15		+ 7
				− 78
turning onto Crête de Saleina			1319	
	0.20	2.35		− 132
pasture			1187	
	0.10	2.45		− 36
Praz de Fort			1151	
	0.08	2.53		− 34
les Arlaches			1117	
	0.12	3.05		− 62
Issert			1055	
	1.00	4.05		+ 271
				− 2
l'Affe			1324	
	0.20	4.25		+ 153
Champex			1477	
			totals:	+ 445
				− 563

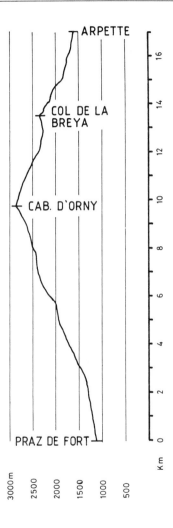

PRAZ de FORT to ARPETTE
by way of the cabane d'Orny
7hrs. 30 mins. 17km

	Timings		Altitude in Metres	Ascent & Descent
	Sectional	Accumul-ative		
Praz de Fort			1151	
	1.10	1.10		+199
path start from road			approx 1350	
	3.15	4.25		+1481
cab d'Orny			2831	
	1.30	5.55		+42
				−472
col de la Breya			2401	
	1.35	7.30		−774
Arpette			1627	
			totals:	+1722
				−1246

7: La FOULY to CHAMPEX/ARPETTE

Walking from la Fouly to Champex will not be too demanding and represents another relatively easy day. The route can be lengthened slightly, and to some advantage, by proceeding beyond Champex and entering the val d'Arpette as far as the Relais d'Arpette. It is an interesting day nevertheless and the intimacy with the (Swiss) val Ferret is particularly pleasant.

For those with surplus energy, and the necessary experience, it is possible to reach the vicinity of Champex by way of the Saleina defile and to visit the d'Orny refuge and possibly, the Trient refuge as well. This really is a 'high route' but if it is to be attempted it would be best for the preceding day to be lengthened and to feature Praz de Fort as the overnight venue. To attempt to walk as far as Praz de Fort on the same day as turning up the Saleina is not a combination that marries very well. For those not too concerned about walking *every* pace of the TMB then the bus will serve admirably for the link between la Fouly and Praz de Fort.

* * *

There are three ways to descend the valley as far as Praz de Fort. The bus has just been mentioned. Then there is a path that comes and goes as it tumbles roughly down the middle of the valley, cutting across the twisting roadway to create a more direct route than that afforded the motorist. Thirdly, there is a rather pleasant path which keeps well away from the fumes and noise of the vehicles.

This path hugs the base of the LH mountainside and starts at the far side of the campsite. To reach the campsite at **la Fouly** it is necessary to leave the village and go down the slip road (past the Information Office) and cross the bridge (the one you will have seen on the LHS as you came down the road from la Ferret). Access to the campsite is made by crossing this bridge, turning first R and continuing over another bridge then go diagonally across the campsite. The waymarking appears to be a yellow diamond edged with a thick black line, mostly in the form of nailed tinplate signs. Alternatively it is labelled as 'chemin pedestre'. For some long distance, it would seem that the campsite utilizes most of the clearings on either side of the track and these secluded pitches look most inviting.

In 45mins there is a junction at a clearing (indication for the village Prayon, over bridge to R), but keep to LHS of river. The path continues to cut through light forest and gives glimpses of the river which sometimes is quite close at hand. Another junction at 40mins where RH turn is signposted for 'le Relais de Branche, cuisine, dortoir & chambres' (*cuisine* = kitchen = food). Nice to know such a place exists, but your route continues, as before, along the LHS of the river. In another 7mins the wide path curves down to R, but take care to go sharp L here onto a minor path (waymarked) which soon presents some interesting footholds where it has been cut into the cliffside. Metallic handrails cater for the squeamish. Coincident with this spot the river takes a picturesque turn as it curves past the base of the cliff.

In about 30mins you should reach a T-junction signposted: 'Praz de Fort/Champex' where turn R onto an impressive path which goes along the Crête de Saleina. *Crête* means crest or ridge and so this will probably be the lateral moraine created by the glacier that issued from the Saleina defile and which retracted a long time ago. The path dips and in 15mins reaches a bridge over the main torrent. Do not cross the bridge but follow the signs leading L to cross the meadows spreading at the foot of the defile. It takes only a matter of moments to pass the scattered chalets at Chanton that merge into those at Praz de Fort.

The path enters **Praz de Fort** alongside the Hôtel Saleinaz which advertises dortoirs. There is a village store to its left and another to the right, adjacent to the Post Office. A lot of people fail to notice the waymarks leading through the village and go L down the road to Issert. This road has no verges and so the walking is not only unpleasant but dangerous. What a contrast is the path linking the two places! This starts on the other side of the road from the Post Office, signposted 'Champex', immediately becoming a path that makes you feel good. It goes parallel to the road, of which you are no longer aware, and in 10mins passes through the most charming little hamlet of **les Arlaches**. After this Issert can be seen and the path gradually curves round and lowers towards it, crossing the bridge and ending at the roadway. There doesn't seem to be any accommodation at **Issert**, although a bar keeps open throughout the day and looks as though tablecloths could appear at lunchtime.

Walk down the road to R and a few paces after the last house you will see the path cutting up L signposted 'Champex 2h'. Two hours is a generous timing and it should be possible even for the weary to improve on this. After such a lengthy and gentle descent from la Fouly, the change of gear seems to strain the legs into that dull feeling of tiredness but, other than that, the walk has its pleasures. Most notable of all will be the view over the small town of Orsières which sits astride the junction of the road coming down the val Ferret and that of the Entremont, the latter being the one which takes the heavy load of the Grand Saint Bernard traffic. Fifty-five minutes to the private chalets of l'Affe and then only another 20mins to get to the lakeside - the lovely lakeside - at **Champex**. In fact, the lake is the nicest feature of the place, around which everything is oh-so-neatly laid out and constructed. Looking behind, the prominent peak in the background is, once again, the Gd. Combin. Champex is a much respected Swiss mountain resort and the usual facilities prevail: hotels, shops, bank, tourist office. Buses come up the multi-hairpinned road from Orsières where they tie in with the timetable schedules of the small-gauge railway linking it with the main line trains at Martigny.

If you are in need of a dortoir then there is the very suitable Chalet en Plein Air: hardly a chalet but seemingly converted from a hotel of the grand style, which offers 42 places in dortoirs with traditional bedrooms as well. This is higher up the village, on its main street. Further on and at the highest end you will see the Camping des Rocailes campsite on the R. You (and the weather) will have to decide on which route you wish to take on the following day: Forclaz by way of the Fenêtre d'Arpette or do you want to go via the Bovine? See the next section for more detailed information that might sway your decision, but consider the following: going via the Bovine will make a stay in Champex the best choice. There are numerous restaurants from which to choose your evening meal and there is plenty to see. You might even be one of the few who run round the lake before breakfast! It is an ideal stopping-off point.

Those wanting to go by the Fenêtre will certainly find that the hotel and dortoir establishment at **Arpette** offers a better start for that route. The Relais d'Arpette, as it is called, can cater for a lot of people and is idyllically situated just at the treeline, facing up the Arpette valley. The way to this place starts by a path which goes into the woods adjacent to the chair-lift base station (a few minutes across the road from the campsite). There is a jeep road going from the same location that also goes to Arpette, signposted 'Fenêtre d'Arpette/la Forclaz', but you will be cheating yourself if you choose to plod up that. The path is one of the most pleasant and you will immediately discover the appeal of the crystal-clear water which tumbles down the channel parallel to it. At places the trees have been thinned on the RHS and there are tempting views to be had towards Martigny. The waymarks are dark green splodges: keep on the path until you have to cross L at a small sluice. Up slightly and R to cross the torrent in the other direction and then L over it again, where immediately turn R and go up with the tumbling waters on your R to meet the road a few paces short of the hotel which you will already have seen through the trees. Twenty-five minutes in all.

PRAZ DE FORT to ARPETTE by way of CABANE D'ORNY

This will be found to be a most demanding and strenuous mountain walk and is the domain of the more energetic and experienced mountain walker. The author only has experience of this alternative route in the opposite direction, so the quoted timings can only be estimates although the exertions are probably comparable. The route allows access to the hotel at Arpette without going through the resort of Champex and this is achieved by way of the col de la Breya, considered by many as being the most difficult pass associated with walking routes in the Mont Blanc area. The initial drop from the col de la Breya is certainly not a *path* and verges on the techniques associated with mountaineering rather than mountain walking.

The upper aiming point is the cabane d'Orny but it is possible to go even higher to visit the wondrous cabane du Trient. 'Wondrous' because of its excellent position on the edge of the enormous Trient glacial plateau. It would be foolhardy for anyone to go right up to the Trient refuge and still expect to be down at the Relais d'Arpette the same evening, although feasible enough for someone going only as far as the d'Orny refuge.

* * *

Praz de Fort is the starting point and every effort should be made to stay in this village during the preceding night as this will allow an advisable early departure. Just to emphasize the demands: the cabane d'Orny is 1,680m (5,512ft) above Praz de Fort but going to the cabane du Trient will involve a climb of 2,029m (6,657ft)!

Go along the side of the Hôtel Saleinaz and curve L following the waymarks. This will lead up past chalets to the centre of the pastures and turn R when the opportunity presents itself to get on a narrow road leading up through the trees and obviously heading for the defile. This gains height monotonously and will probably take some 45mins before it starts to zig-zag. The wanted path starts from the top of an embankment which runs along the RHS of the road, the point of access to it being somewhat ill-defined although there may be a dilapidated and half-hidden sign 'ORNY' to indicate the spot. Once found, the path starts its own zig-zagging, subsequently sweeping L to commence an upward trail over a lengthy scree-covered slope. Whilst this is going on the pleasures of the opposing mountainside are gathering in magnitude. After some 40mins the contributory defile coming down from the left will come into line and permit distant sightings up to the enormous mountain wall blocking its upper reaches. The tail of the Saleina glacier tumbles down here and you should be able to see the cab. de Saleina perched precariously on a little barren shelf up on the left and be able to trace the path leading to it.

Higher up still the monolith on the left becomes dominant and its slowly changing shape is intriguing: the Clochers du Portalet. From leaving the roadway, it will probably have taken two hours to draw level with the end of the glacier d'Orny and the immediate landscape is moon-like: desolate, rugged and gaunt. From this vicinity it should be possible to see the new steep-roofed **refuge d'Orny**. Note that it is situated alongside the upper of the two nearby lakes: on some maps it is shown by the lower lake which represented the position of the older and smaller refuge which was

91

demolished by avalanche. Fortunately the opportunity was taken in constructing the new one to improve on its size and facilities and, in consequence, lunches and evening meals are available. It can probably cater for about eighty visitors in its dormitories.

The path sweeps to the L at the junction with a path coming up from the R: this is where you will have to return if you are visiting the refuge as it marks the start of the way to the col de la Breya.

The position of the refuge is highly attractive and there is usually a handful of people sitting on the uncomfortable concrete wall outside, casually absorbing the beautiful scenery which starts with the unbelievably-blue water of the adjacent lake and then scans the immediate horizon with bigger mountains to be seen in the distance over to the left.

Having got this far and liked it, why not go even higher? The **cabane du Trient** cannot be seen from the d'Orny but is positioned just round to the right of the upper limits of the mountain wall running behind the refuge. The approach will take some 1hr 15mins and sets off from the front of the d'Orny refuge, where the path drops down to skirt the LHS of the lake and then branches slightly L to get to the (usually) snow-covered glacier. There is normally a trodden path to follow which keeps well over towards the RH wall. Whilst this is regarded as a 'safe' glacier, there are crevasses, although these are narrow enough to cross with a degree of care and are sometimes marked for greater awareness. The guardian of the d'Orny refuge should be consulted before embarking on this little glacial venture and will give his opinion. At a point approaching an obvious swing from the right in the glacier's progression, there is a turn to R (usually indicated by a marker pole) which leads over to the rocks.

A path then climbs the mountainside, turning to cross an exposed patch before going through a defile whereupon the cabane du Trient is found along with its magnificent views. To stay a night here will add a day to your Tour but surely it would be well worth it? What a magnificent position it is in, surrounded by all the glory of the true high Alps. The great snowfield which dominates the foreground is known as the Plâteau du Trient, obviously easing its

The col du Grand Ferret (Stage 6) (Photo: R.B. Evans)

Descent from the col du Grand Ferret towards La Fouly *(Stage 6)*
Old houses at Issert (Stage 7)   (Photos: R.B.Evans)

way down L to become the glacier d'Orny but its greatest movement is probably to the R where it issues as the glacier du Trient, the downpouring of which is best seen after crossing the Fenêtre d'Arpette (see later). The cabane du Trient is credited as being one of Switzerland's most prestigious huts and to sit outside watching the dusk descend to a point of total darkness is probably only matched by the coming of the dawn.

Eventually it will be necessary to retrace your way back to the d'Orny and the path junction slightly beyond. Branch L here and descend through a rocky chasm known as the Combe d'Orny and head over towards the obvious lower exit gap. Here a path goes R down the RH flank towards Som le Proz and Orsières but be careful to ignore that one and to branch L, keeping generally level. After about 20mins branch L again and climb slightly, away from the path that heads towards la Breya and Grands Plans where the upper station of the chair-lift cableway coming from Champex is located.

At the **col de la Breya** the way down goes sharply L over the ridge although the 'arrival' path continues further for an undefined distance. When last there the col was indicated as such. As mentioned earlier, the Arpette side of the col is fairly vicious and it will take some 15mins before the going becomes more agreeable. The route then descends through rock-strewn upper valleys before dropping below the treeline and eventually reaching the bottom of the val d'Arpette at a point some 10mins above the **Relais d'Arpette**, so turn R after crossing the stream to get to it.

The considerations for the ensuing day and whether it is to be over the Fenêtre or by way of the Bovine will influence where you spend the night. If you want to go to Champex then either descend by the jeep track or go down the forest path which starts on the LHS of the jeep track immediately after the hotel: by either way it should take no longer than 25mins. The type of person coming over the route just described is hardly likely to be attracted to the tranquillity of the Bovine and will doubtless be a candidate for the Fenêtre d'Arpette, in which case he will find himself ideally positioned at the Relais d'Arpette.

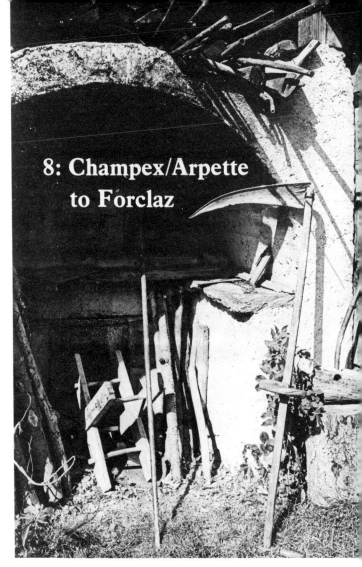

8: Champex/Arpette to Forclaz

An old farmhouse

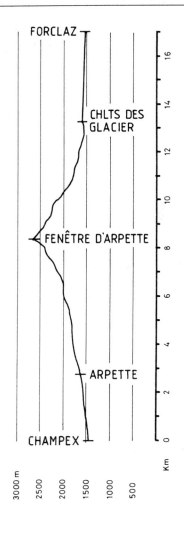

CHAMPEX to la FORCLAZ
by way of the Fenêtre d'Arpette
6hrs. 15mins. 17km

	Timings		Altitude in Metres	Ascent & Descent
	Sectional	Accumul-ative		
Champex			1477	
	0.30	0.30		+ 150
Arpette			1627	
	1.40	2.10		+ 473
path junction			2100	
	1.20	3.30		+ 565
Fenêtre d'Arpette			2665	
	1.00	4.30		− 569
ruined chalets			2096	
	1.00	5.30		− 513
chlt des Glacier			1583	
	0.45	6.15		− 57
la Forclaz			1526	
			totals:	+ 1188
				− 1139

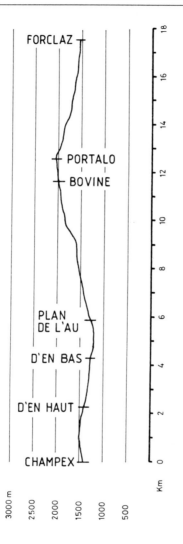

FORCLAZ

PORTALO
BOVINE

PLAN
DE L'AU

D'EN BAS

D'EN HAUT

CHAMPEX

3000 m 2500 2000 1500 1000 500

Km   0   2   4   6   8   10   12   14   16   18

CHAMPEX to la FORCLAZ
by way of Bovine
4hrs. 30mins. 17.5km

| | Timings | | Altitude in Metres | Ascent & Descent |
	Sectional	Accumulative		
Champex			1477	
	0.25	0.25		+ 15
				− 48
Champex d'en Haut			1444	
	0.25	0.50		− 122
adj Champex d'en Bas			1322	
	0.20	1.10		+ 8
plan de l'Au			1330	
	1.35	2.45		+ 573
emerge to pasture			1903	
	0.25	3.10		+ 84
Bovine			1987	
	0.15	3.25		+ 62
ridge			2049	
	1.05	4.30		− 523
la Forclaz			1526	
			totals:	+ 742
				− 693

8: CHAMPEX/ARPETTE to FORCLAZ

Why la Forclaz? Others will be aiming for Trient, so why not there? Well, everything is possible, but the author believes an overnight at Forclaz will allow the ensuing day to produce greater return both in terms of the visual prospects and the walking potential.

As stated at the end of the preceding section, a decision has to be made between the two alternative routes that link Champex with Forclaz. Although the less dramatic of the two, the Bovine route is of immense beauty and should not just be regarded as the way to go only if bad weather is threatening the Fenêtre d'Arpette. With clarity it is able to produce extensive views along the Rhône valley and the mountainous terrain surrounding Martigny. Taking less time than the Arpette route, it is by no means a stroll and whilst it is true that both have their distinctive attractions, the way via the Fenêtre will remain the brute challenge for the experienced walker.

For those who might toy with the idea of walking both these routes to get to Forclaz, the solution is simple. After the first night at Forclaz take an early bus in the morning to Martigny. The bus terminates outside the main railway station, allowing about 5mins to get a ticket and board the awaiting small-gauge train for Orsières. The 30mins train ride is very pleasant. At Orsières there will be a connecting bus for the exciting hairpin ascent to Champex. Square one! When purchasing the ticket at Martigny, book straight through to Champex.

* * *

The Fenêtre route is a demanding and rugged mountain trail and the jewel in its crown will become obvious upon arrival at the col as the immense glacier du Trient suddenly comes on display. It is a very engaging mountain walk, starting very passively at the **Arpette** hotel where an early departure is advisable. Up the wide central track, then onto a much narrower path in 35mins. This path drifts over to the RHS and takes 45mins to reach the commencement of a rocky chasm. Take care to turn sharp R immediately after the chasm, 20mins, although the turning is usually clearly indicated. It is at this path junction that you have the first proper glimpse of the col you are aiming for (it is the lowest notch on the skyline ridge to the R of the dark spikey crags). After the path has gained height for 25mins, rounding a corner will allow the opportunity for a more detailed impression of the col which is noticeably closer. The rock wall on the R is made attractive by a covering of yellow-green lichen.

Shortly after this the path negotiates a rocky area and then, 35mins, boulders are encountered where progress must be monitored with the utmost care. Do try to keep to the general line indicated by the paint splashes. The boulders are surprisingly stable but be vigilant for the odd rogue. You will suddenly find yourself confronted with the final climb, up which there are many criss-crossing tracks. Late-lying snow may be nestling in the gully at the foot of the slope but it is usually easy to cross. With sure footing and a modicum of determination it should then take no more than 20mins to get to the top and to chalk up another col to your credit. The views to both sides of the **Fenêtre d'Arpette** are far reaching and will be a satisfying reward for the expended effort. It is here that you will have your introduction to the glacier du Trient, the might and splendour of which will only become fully apparent during the 2-hour descent alongside it.

The author has never seen the danger for himself, but the route over the Fenêtre is marked on most maps as being treacherous or difficult, so a cautionary word is warranted. The valley is well known for its avalanche dangers, but these should be clear by the earliest time recommended for a clear-round Tour. Danger would certainly lurk for the unwary if snow was packed deceptively between the numerous rocks and a twisted or broken ankle would be an abrupt and painful end to anyone's holiday.

The descent looks ominous but, like most challenges, proves easier in the event although care is the obvious byword. It is steep in places and a walking stick or ice-axe can be of immense help at such times. In an hour the path goes past the remains of some stone buildings, destroyed to a point that they look only like a stubby wall. It is from just here that the glacier has better visual balance: quite often its lower reaches are used for exercises by small contingents of Swiss troops and only when you see them on the ice is the true scale of the glacier's immensity brought home. From here a further hour will bring you down to a collection of buildings known as **Chlt. du Glacier.** Here there is a modern, but private, refuge in addition to a lockable lean-to which dispenses fizzy drinks, beer and biscuits to very grateful customers. This spot is probably coincident with the point of 'optimum thirst' on this particular stage, so its presence has an important role to play!

A fraction beyond the shacks is a bridge, the crossing of which is featured in the following section. For now, keep on the RHS of the river by joining the path going directly to Forclaz. This path is unique in the Mont Blanc region because it has for company one of the finest working examples of a *bisse*. A *bisse* is an almost horizontal open channel which carries water to where it is required from some distant source. The path winds round the tree-clad mountainside and the shade makes it nice and cool, with the fresh smell of pine. At clearings it is possible to look down onto Trient set in a valley deep below and study the opposing mountainside where the refuge at col de Balme can be seen at the head of the only major defile. The walk takes 45mins finishing at the road col at **Forclaz** where there is an able hotel. Whilst traditional rooms are available, its second floor is devoted to dortoir accommodation: meals and bar service. There is also a shop selling basic foodstuffs and other useful commodities as well as souvenir items. There is an overflow dortoir opposite the main building and tenting is possible with permission. There is an infrequent bus service operating from Martigny which continues to the lower village of Trient and the frontier village of le Châtelard.

* * *

THE BOVINE ROUTE

Adjacent to the chair-lift base station at the upper end of **Champex** there is also a sign: 'Plan de l'Au, Bovine, col de la Forclaz'. Proceed along the roadway and in 9mins take LH turn down narrow road, indicated 'Vallon de Champex'. The Sunways hotel is the striking feature just here and its location appears ideal and tranquil. Follow the road as it curves R, passing numerous holiday chalets which are made to look additionally attractive with baskets of geraniums hanging from their eaves. This is a very pleasant path and where it draws parallel with a stream in a large meadow, watch out for LH turn, 23mins from the hotel, indicated: 'Plan de l'Au, Bovine, Forclaz'. The path enters woodland with moss-covered rocks and ferns. The waymark appears to be the yellow diamond framed in black.

The shacks at **plan de l'Au**, 18mins, offer no service to the passer-by. It is then a jeep track for 20mins obviously created to aid forestry work, but at the limit of this the continuing pleasant path reaches a clearing in an additional 5mins with good views to the valley. A fierce torrent is crossed at 17mins and then the path levels (relatively speaking) to cross three minor torrents.

Now the bad news. From here on the path climbs steeply and relentlessly for some 30mins to surmount the hillside that has faced you for some little while. Once above the treeline, though, it becomes a different world and the unobstructed views are particularly good. Continue in the same general direction for 5mins to where there is a refreshing cool stream which can be of service to tired feet. The path goes R here to contour round the slopes of the grassy mountainside for 25mins to reach the cattle sheds and unoccupied chalets at **Bovine**. Along this stretch the most far-reaching views along the Rhône valley beyond Martigny are a delight. It is possible to see the length of the val Ferret with the glacier suspended high on the ridge which separates it from the val Entremont.

It is easy to get the impression that Forclaz cannot be far away, but a glance at the map will show Bovine as being only midway. But the difficulties are over as, apart from the 15mins it takes to get up to the gate/fence at the small ridge, it is a very easy and pleasant downhill walk all the way to the Forclaz hotel, 1hr 15mins. As the path drops, the sightings of Martigny, hundreds of feet lower, are intriguing and the wide zig-zagging scar of the highway coming up to the **col de la Forclaz** vividly illustrates the skills and determination of the road builder. The hotel looks only moments away at times, but after successive corner turning you eventually learn to be patient.

Sheds at Bovine are reported as having been converted into dortoir accommodation but no further detail is known.

The Chamonix valley from the Col de Balme

9: Forclaz to Trélechamp

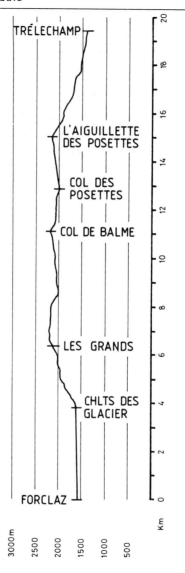

la FORCLAZ to TRÉLECHAMP
6hrs. 19.4km

| | Timings | | Altitude | Ascent |
	Sectional	Accumul-ative	in Metres	& Descent
la Forclaz			1526	
	0.45	0.45		+ 57
chlt des Glacier			1583	
	1.25	2.10		+ 530
les Grands			2113	
	0.08	2.18		+ 32
highest point			approx 2145	
	1.27	3.45		+ 73
				− 27
col de Balme			2191	
	0.30	4.15		+ 5
				− 199
col des Posettes			1997	
	0.35	4.50		+ 204
l'Aiguillette des Posettes			2201	
	1.10	6.00		− 801
Trélechamp			1400	
		totals:		+ 901
				− 1027

Deviation to ALBERT 1er refuge from COL de BALME
4hrs. 50mins. 12.6km

	Timings		Altitude in Metres	Ascent & Descent
	Sectional	Accumulative		
col de Balme			2191	
	0.10	0.10		− 1
bubblecar station			2190	
	0.20	0.30		+ 81
lac de Charamillon			2271	
	0.15	0.45		+ 58
corner			2329	
	1.05	1.50		+ 377
				− 4
Albert 1er refuge			2702	
	3.00	4.50		+ 5
				− 516
col de Balme			2191	
			totals:	+ 521
				− 521

9: la FORCLAZ to TRÉLECHAMP

The *bisse* path leading to Chlt. du Glacier starts across the road from the hotel at **Forclaz**, signposted: 'les Grands, col de Balme'. It takes 45mins to walk its length and is a gentle start to the day. Approximately half-way, at a clearing, an unrestricted view up to the Balme refuge will show the main target of the day: it sits in the dip at the head of the opposing ravine.

Having reached **Chlt. du Glacier**, cross the bridge and turn L at the T-junction, signposted: left for 'les Grands, col de Balme', right for 'Trient'. The path L twists and turns to gain height up the thinly-wooded slopes, permitting attractive sightings of the Trient glacier. At a bend, the view extends over the glacier and it is just possible to trace the line of the path coming down from the Fenêtre d'Arpette which looks aggressively difficult from this standpoint. The path soon gets its head above the treeline and the gentle curves twist through pleasant shrubland, culminating at the base of a staircase created at a diagonal fault in the RH rockwall. The loose handrails offer some consolation and once at the top it is only a few paces to the couple of shacks that are collectively known as **les Grands**, 1hr 24mins.

One of the buildings has been turned into a private summer residence and by the plastic covered notice on display it is obvious that the passing mountain walker is unwelcome: in French, of course, but 'don't do this, don't do that, etc.' It is a charming little spot but spoilt by this display of hostility. It used to be an ideal bivouac location and certainly a place to linger, but it is probably best to carry on without a halt, the path continuing diagonally up the slopes behind the buildings.

After a short while, the path has several short up and down sections which average out to become a most wonderful balcony path. There is no way off this path until reaching the col de Balme, so be content to meander its course. It follows the sweep of several curves and the belief that the refuge must be just round the next bend is proved false time and again: very tantalising. The *bisse* path from Forclaz can easily be recognised, now far below, its clear line raking the hillside above the village of Trient. There is a waterfall about half-way along, its cool tumbling waters spreading over smooth black rock. The pools could have remedial effect on weary feet, and, if it wasn't for the fear of people coming round the corner…!

More or less straight ahead, the near end of the massif comprising the Dents du Midi is the bulk that draws the eye. Eventually the turn is made that contours the final hillside to lead to the refuge, a safe and secure path in the absence of snow. Caution must be exercised in crossing any patches of snow which usually lie in steepish rakes that descend a long way below the path level and can create awkward diversions. Arrival at the **col de Balme** is a highly rewarding experience: there's the refuge with its comforts, a gaggle of other walkers to add a bit of life to the occasion and, above all, the glorious scenery that fills the whole of the valley ahead. Most notable is the near-at-hand Aig. Verte, 4,122m (13,523ft), with the adjacent Dru, 3,754m (12,316ft). In the distance, the white dagger reaching for the valley is the glacier des Bossons of which you will see a lot more during the ensuing days. Mont Blanc is way in the distance, but it crowns the range to give it a balanced perspective.

The Balme refuge is run by a lady who has changed little over the years. She rules the procession of her customers with a firm hand: arrive late and you get no lunch, although snacks would still be available. On the other side of the coin, she does a superb egg and bacon. Spend the night here by all means if only to avail yourself of the toilet (best seen by fumbling torchlight), when you can experience at first hand the facilities generally endured by your forefathers.

Relaxing at the col de Balme is highly satisfying, but the TMB beckons. The intention is to walk to the col des Montets by the Posettes route and there is a sign outside the refuge indicating the way. The path dips into the little hollow behind the refuge, then contours the mountainside, eventually bearing L and dipping to where there is a little circular lake, 20mins, and a further 8mins to the **col Posettes**. At this junction of paths the aim is to proceed diagonally L from the line of approach and certainly not taking the level path which kisses the chalets further to the L. The required path climbs a grassy bank and then twists and turns as it gets noticeably rocky.

From the col there is a sighting of the massive concrete wall of the Emosson barrage, holding back the enormous volume of water that is a contributing source of power for one of Switzerland's largest hydro-electric schemes. Climbing higher than the col will show the surface of the restrained water and give a better impression of the scale of the enterprise.

As you will discover, the path is superb. The way it dodges along a ridge here and a miniature cleft there is just a delight. Each stone, each rock, each bush, each flower, each little black lake seems to have been put in position with some divine care and there is no doubt in the author's mind that this is *the* path of the region. Notwithstanding the path itself, it happens to offer the most wonderful views ahead to the main Mont Blanc range along with the most glorious study of the wide suspended glacier du Tour on the L and oversees the valley on the RHS in which le Buet and Vallorcine nestle.

The path worms its way without losing any of its attraction until drawing level with the summit of l'Aiguillette des Posettes, 33mins. The path begins a series of drops from here and in only 4mins ignore LH turn and carry straight on, indicated: 'Col des Montets par l'Arette - TMB'. After some little while, the path goes as far as it dares to the RH edge of the tumbling mountainside and from here there is an impression to be gained of the ascending path linking the col des Montets with the approach to lac Blanc and la Flégère as it scales the corner wall of the Aiguilles Rouges, a sight that will make you flinch from the task of scaling it later on.

Shortly after this, the path dips fiercely to L to encounter a path junction, 30mins, where turn sharp R to continue the descent. By now in dense woodland and the boots slipping on the exposed tree roots that ruck the path, turn R at each of the successive junctions until reaching the road just below the col des Montets, 26mins. There is a path running parallel to the road and the path coming down to this forms a T-junction, indicated: L for 'Trélechamp' / R for 'Col des Montets'. The building at col des Montets is that associated with the Natural Park of the Aiguilles Rouges (opening hours: 10 to 6) with displays of stuffed mountain animals, illustrated literature, maps and other general information. It does offer a bar service, the availability of toilets being an additional and notable attraction. The backpacker might like to know that 'wild' bivouacking is allowed on the grassy area just over the col and to R, where a clear stream enhances the value of the pitch.

Those wanting more secure accommodation for the night will find it necessary to turn L and go to **Trélechamp** where there is a very good gîte d'étape, la Boerne, 5mins, 37 places. This is a most engaging establishment, which can be singled out as the shining example of how a good guardian can really lift what might otherwise be an ordinary occasion into a pleasant experience. The bedding is comfortable, the food prepared with pride and the washing/shower/toilet facilities as good as one would hope. As these complimentary remarks are bound to prove an anti-climax to the sceptical, there are other places to stay, notably at **Argentière**, a very large and attractive village some 25mins down the path which runs parallel to the stream outside the gîte.

Argentière has numerous hotels and restaurants, a Tourist Office and Post Office. On the main road, buses link it to Chamonix, as does the narrow-gauge railway: the station can be found at the lower end of the village. There are numerous shops but the one of most interest will be the supermarket that is hidden from view under the terrace of shops at the highest end of the village, also accessible from behind the Post Office. Argentière has a gîte d'étape called Gîte le Belvédère.

* * *

From the **col de Balme**, the traditional TMB route runs straight down the centre of the valley below the refuge, passing the bubblecar intermediate station at Charamillon, 32mins, and getting to the cable-car base station at le Tour in a further 25mins. This route has fallen into decline because of the extensive ski-lift systems that have ruined the environment. The path itself is quite substantial and mention is made of its continued existence in case bad weather creates the need for an alternative to the Posettes route which would be more exposed in adverse conditions. The effects of exposure to the elements would certainly be lessened. For the second half of the drop, take care to get onto the path which starts along the LHS of the large bubblecar interchange station.

At the LHS of the base station in **le Tour** is the Olympique two-star hotel which will provide immediate relief to the weary and by booking in here you could be up to your neck in scalding bath water within minutes. It is certainly the largest hotel in this small village, where there are only a few smaller and cheaper places to stay. The food is superb. Le Tour is a very pretty village and exploration of its narrow streets is well worthwhile: every other wooden house appears to have a hanging basket filled with geraniums giving spikey bursts of red colour. There is an enormous Club Alpin Français (CAF) building at the far end of a small road going L through the centre of the village although the right of access to this is uncertain but possibly worth personal investigation (the author has had a friendly reception at the place and been served with their meals without question).

Just next to the hotel is the bar/basic store la Chaumière which might offer all the facilities you need before continuing down the road to **Montroc**, 18mins. The bus running the length of the Chamonix valley floor (Chamonix Bus) has its upper terminus outside the cableway station at le Tour and this runs down through Montroc and Argentière. At Montroc, its central feature is the twee railway station, through which the trains coming from Vallorcine and the Swiss frontier emerge from the tunnel and descend to Argentière and Chamonix. There seem to be no other facilities in Montroc and the one hotel looks too expensive to contemplate.

A decision must be made as to whether you continue on the original TMB path to **Trélechamp**, 15mins by way of a path which goes over the tunnel portal, or go down to Argentière, 20mins by way of road. The refuge le Moulin is run on dortoir lines with the availability of basic evening meals and this is located off a turning to the L some 8mins down the Argentière road.

ALBERT 1er REFUGE from COL DE BALME

Assuming an arrival at the col de Balme around lunchtime, why not consider a visit to the Albert 1er refuge? ('1er' is an abbreviation for *premier* which means '1st'. The refuge was named after a Belgian king who was a keen mountaineer and frequent visitor to the region). It would not take more than two hours to get there and would possibly be a memorable overnight. It is situated right next to the massive and rucked surface of the glacier du Tour and it is this glacier, rather than anything else, that is the 'star turn'.

111

To go up to the hut and then down to the valley in one trip would be too much for the average walker. Staying there would allow the subsequent day to be fairly easy, returning to Balme and rejoining the TMB to Trélechamp by the Posettes route.

So, a visit to the Albert 1er refuge would add a day to the itinerary but you are strongly advised to do this if you sense the likelihood of having time in hand when you reach les Houches. If time dictates a choice between the Aig. du Midi cable-car and the Albert 1er, then the Midi would win due to the glory of its panoramic terraces. Similarly, if you have visited the Trient refuge then the Albert 1er is less of an attraction by comparison, but if you only got to the d'Orny then the prospect of going to Albert 1er should have some reward. Seen from the refuge, the close view of the deeply-crevassed glacier surface is impressive, although it is only when you happen to spot the minuscular dots of mountaineers doing a bit of icework that the enormity of the thing becomes apparent.

* * *

The path to be taken is the one heading along to the left in the direction of the **Balme** cableway station, 10mins. Pass just to the L of the station to reach the narrow outpouring from lac de Charamillon, 20mins. Then continue on the almost-level path as it follows the curve of the hillside which has its share of alpine flowers. An ermine was seen on this flank during one of the author's visits - what a privilege! Thought at first to be a squirrel, its lower and slimmer body looked almost silver as the fur took the glint of the sunlight. Marmots also seem to abound just here and you will probably be startled by their sentry's shrill whistle as he warns the others of your intrusion into his territory. Another 5mins to junction of path coming up from R (this comes from the half-way cableway station seen in the middle of the bowl below and could be a convenient escape route on the following day, as the descent to the valley floor would be hastened).

Where the path rounds a shoulder, 15mins, the air seems to drop ten degrees in temperature - but it's probably only psychological as the massive glacier du Tour comes on display. The amazing sight of all that ice will create yet another dimension to your catalogue of

Albert Premier refuge at dawn, with the sun striking the summit of the Aiguille Verte

memories. The path turns to the L, climbing occasionally, taking 15mins to reach the last promontory before negotiating a delicate little defile facilitated with a steel cable handrail. The refuge can be seen sitting on a shelf up on the left but it will take almost an hour to reach it.

The path goes R to cross a well-trodden course over a scree field to reach the glacier's lateral moraine, where the path turns L to go upwards along its crest. The final approach becomes comparatively steep. The refuge is very substantial and can accommodate lots of visitors. Meals are provided at mid-day and during the evening. The **Albert 1er** is a very popular refuge and an ideal base for climbing parties setting off for the many magnificent routes ranged around. It is usual for overnight boarders to be allocated dormitories associated with certain times of rousing the next morning so if you don't want to be awakened until 7.00am make sure you are not in with a lot who've asked for a 3.00am shaking!

Although the more modern stone-built premises close earlier than expected in season, the adjacent and much older wooden refuge is kept open for a little longer on a do-it-yourself basis. In late season it would obviously be prudent to ensure you have adequate food stocks to safeguard such an eventuality. In any case, do go and inspect the older place as it has a charm all its own.

Retracing the path is simplicity itself although care must be taken if overnight frost or a sprinkling of snow have made the slope under the refuge a little treacherous.

Behind the refuge one of the novelties of the Alps can be seen - do look for it. Just below the jagged summit of the Aig. du Tour there is a precariously perched gigantic flat boulder. It is called the Table de Roc.

*Aiguille Verte and the Drus from la Floria restaurant
between la Flégère and Chamonix*

10: Trélechamp to la Flégère

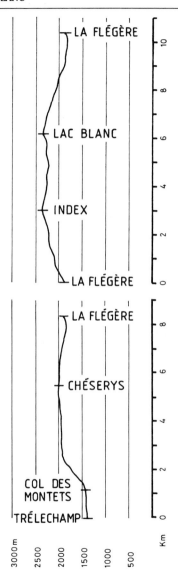

TRÉLECHAMP to la FLÉGÈRE
3hrs. 10mins. 8.3km

	Timings		Altitude in Metres	Ascent & Descent
	Sectional	Accumul-ative		
Trélechamp			1400	
	0.20	0.20		+61
col des Montets			1461	
	1.55	2.15		+599
highest point			2060	
	0.15	2.30		−62
chlt des Chéserys			1998	
	0.40	3.10		+18
				−139
la Flégère			1877	
			totals:	+678
				−201

Visit to LAC BLANC from la FLÉGÈRE
3hrs. 10mins. 10.3km

	Timings		Altitude in Metres	Ascent & Descent
la Flégère			1877	
(by foot)	1.05	1.05		+508
Index			2385	
	1.10	2.15		+19
				−52
lac Blanc			2352	
	0.55	3.10		+9
				−484
la Flégère			1877	
			totals:	+536
				−536

10: TRÉLECHAMP to la FLÉGÈRE

The route from Trélechamp/col des Montets to les Houches described in the next two stages skirts the flanks of the range known as the *Aiguilles Rouges*. The scenic potential along this section of the TMB stands comparison with anything that might have given delight thus far and, once at height, the ever-changing aspects afforded by progressing the route will unfold to reveal exquisite views to the main chain on the opposing side of the valley. It's impossible to single out any one viewpoint as 'offering the best', but a strong contender would have to be the spot known as lac Blanc which enjoys a well-earned reputation for its setting.

Lac Blanc has a modern refuge that has been constructed 'out of the line of fire' to replace the original smaller one that was destroyed by a succession of avalanches in the late eighties. Here, then, will also be found the amenities of food, drink and lodging which will be of value for those who want them.

When doing the TMB, staying at lac Blanc is all very well but it does impose a certain limitation on the staging of the ensuing day. After la Flégère there is no accommodation until getting to the refuge at Belachat and reaching this at the end of the day should be within everyone's ability. But for those who would want to end their day at les Houches - for whatever reason - walking from lac Blanc might be asking a bit too much, which restricts la Flégère to being the more effectual setting-off point. Remember, too, that the views extending across the valley from the whole length of the Aiguilles Rouges' flanks should be savoured, not rushed.

The suggestion is made that you make straight for la Flégère by way of Chéserys, secure a bedplace in their dortoir and then visit lac Blanc in the afternoon with either a light pack or, better still, no pack at all. The chair-lift system climbing up from Flégère to Index could be an enormous help in the approach to lac Blanc using a splendid high-level path, the return being unaided by the direct diagonal descent.

* * *

It is necessary to get to the road col at Montets, adjacent to which is the path start needed to surmount the north-eastern shoulder of the Aiguilles Rouges. No matter where the night was spent, the way to the col leads through Trélechamp. If the day is started at le Tour, then walk down the road to Montroc and reach Trélechamp by the path which goes over the main railway tunnel portal. If you are quitting Argentière come up the main road and where it veers to the L to commence the zig-zagging watch out for a path at that first corner which goes up to Trélechamp next to the stream.

At the very upper LH corner of **Trélechamp** the paths and tracks come onto the road, but it is necessary to walk along the side of that for a short while until getting onto a parallel path running on the RHS. It comes onto a clearing used as a car park: cross this and walk the length of a pleasant path in what is obviously an alpine garden with every plant and shrub labelled and named. At **col des Montets** cross the road to go along the LHS of the large building and bear L round the curved path for about fifty paces where the path going R to Chéserys, la Flégère and lac Blanc will be found, usually indicated.

The path climbs gently at first, but soon the zig-zags become more compacted as the gradient steepens. It is a very good path, with lots of immediate interest. The little round black berries on the low bushes will not be a new discovery but there are as many concentrated on these slopes as will have been seen previously. They are the *Myrtille* and are particularly tasty, quite often featured as the main ingredient for over-rated and over-priced tarts in the valley restaurants, but here they are free for the taking. After 35mins the path comes to a little clearing on a shoulder, permitting the first of the extensive views along and over the Chamonix valley.

Throughout the Tour, Mont Blanc itself always appears too remote and, with its rounded summit, rather featureless. Consequently, emphasis is always drawn to the surrounding summits which have far more character. The Verte, however, stands alone and can be 'taken in'; as such it is seen to absolute advantage from this balcony route. The immediate terrain is earthy with plenty of smooth boulders to rest against.

There is 45mins of further ascent before the path begins to level in a rock-strewn clearing. With the worst of the climbing accomplished, the walk is much more gentle and, being so exposed, produces the most wonderful views along the main chain on the

119

left. The Mer de Glace glacier is beginning to show itself from behind its barrier walls, leading down past Montenvers. Thirty-five minutes will bring you to a path junction, R to lac Blanc, which ignore if it is your intention to accept the proposals made in the introduction.

A little further on there is a host of path junctions: another R to lac Blanc and one coming up from Argentière. Continue in a generally straight direction through the plateau known as **Chéserys**, skirting along the RHS of the stone building (quite often indistinct due to vegetation). A short while later the small torrent coming from lac Blanc has to be crossed and after this, it takes some 50mins to la Flégère, which can be seen from Chéserys perched on the nose of a descending ridge. Unless visibility is restricted, strolling along this section is particularly rewarding - the views are of the highest order and there is so much to see.

La Flégère offers hotel-style bedrooms in its main building during the summer months but dortoir accommodation is to be found at the older building just below (apply in the restaurant of the upper building beforehand). The capacity is generous, so there should be no difficulty in securing a place.

During the lunch period the restaurant offers a wide and appetizing choice from a self-service counter, but only set meals are provided in the evening. A bar seems to operate throughout the day. So much for the comforts! Now how are you going to spend the rest of the day? If you want to go to lac Blanc, the suggestion is made that you start your approach from **Index** which is 1hr 20mins walk up the tortuous slope behind Flégère: you may not have the time to do this, so why not use the chair-lift facility? The cost for a one-way journey will not be unreasonable and it makes a whole difference to the outing. The path goes R from the upper station and it is easy to follow, although late-lying snow in gullies can be troublesome. It is a superb path, weaving and ducking through the rock-strewn terrain, finally rounding the cliffs of the upper peaks to reach **lac Blanc** in 1hr. Here in the new refuge, you will find every facility for quenching your thirst or having a snack.

Most visitors feel that lac Blanc occupies a unique position along the flanks of the Aiguilles Rouges because of the balanced aspect of the range opposite. The Mer de Glace seems to bisect the range, the

Grandes Jorasses clearly visible at its rear. Aig. Verte and the Drus, along with the Aig. du Chardonnet and the Aig. d'Argentière are to the left. To the right the Chamonix Aiguilles, capped by the Aig. du Midi, which lead to the summit of Mont Blanc and the slightly lower Dôme du Goûter.

The final 2 or 3mins of approach to lac Blanc from Index share the path coming from la Flégère and when the time comes to depart, it is down this same path that you must go. It is a pleasant descent and takes 55mins to get to **Flégère**, the very last part being familiar from the Chéserys approach.

Some people have the notion that it is too expensive to stay at altitude and will scurry down to the valley for overnight accommodation using the Flégère/les Praz cable-car. Of course, it might be their intention to take in a little 'night life', so *good luck* in finding it. Even if it costs more, to stay at height usually has the edge over that obtainable lower down and avoids the need to get back up the following morning, when the time of the first cable-car becomes a restrictive factor. But, even if the cost of accommodation were slightly less, by the time the return cable-car fare is added to the bill...! There is an excellent path descending to Chamonix from la Flégère although the top of it has been desecrated by another of those insidious ski slopes. It passes the balcony restaurant/café at la Floria before continuing to the valley to emerge on the edge of the town near to the hospital.

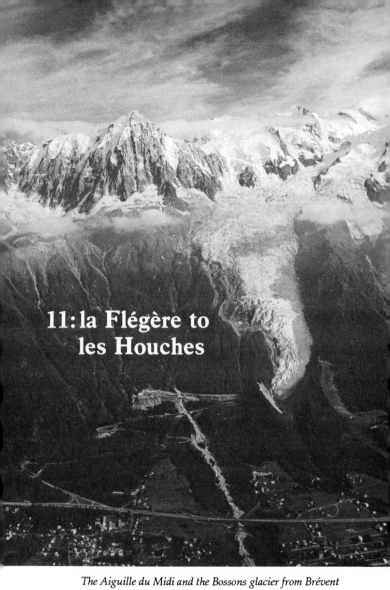

11: la Flégère to les Houches

The Aiguille du Midi and the Bossons glacier from Brévent

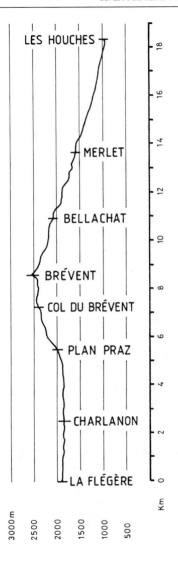

LES HOUCHES

MERLET

BELLACHAT

BRÉVENT

COL DU BRÉVENT

PLAN PRAZ

CHARLANON

LA FLÉGÈRE

Km

3000 m   2500   2000   1500   1000   500

la FLÉGÈRE to les HOUCHES
6hrs. 20 mins. 18.2km

	Timings		Altitude in Metres	Ascent & Descent
	Sectional	Accumul-ative		
la Flégère			1877	
	0.55	0.55		+ 2
				− 67
Charlanon			1812	
	0.50	1.45		+ 201
				− 13
Plan Praz (restaurant)			2000	
	0.50	2.35		+ 368
col du Brévent			2368	
	0.45	3.20		+ 175
				− 18
le Brévent			2525	
	0.55	4.15		+ 8
				− 381
Bellachat			2152	
	1.00	5.15		+ 17
				− 607
Merlet			1562	
	0.45	6.00		− 366
Statue le Christ Roi			1196	
	0.20	6.20		− 216
les Houches, station			980	
			totals:	+ 771
				− 1668

The val d'Arpette (Stage 8)

Aiguille Verte and the Dru seen from Charlanon (stage 11)
At the col du Brévent with Aig. du Midi, Mont Blanc and its glaciers (stage 1
(Photos: A.Harper)

11: La FLÉGÈRE to les HOUCHES

This is it: the last day. A day to cherish if it means being back in your own home the following night and certainly one to remember as the path is exciting with numerous viewpoints of distinction along the way.

It seems as though the management have to wait until the arrival of the first cable-car to obtain fresh bread, causing breakfast at la Flégère to be had at the expense of a not-too-early departure. A good tip is to have all the gear packed so that no time is lost. The walking demands are fairly extensive; most people finding they have had more than enough as they wend their final paces towards les Houches. Time must be allowed for lengthy stops at the many places en route which offer stupendous views, so try to set off as soon as possible.

* * *

From **la Flégère** the small complex at Plan Praz can look deceptively close, but the fact is it will take almost 2hrs to get there. You start to enjoy your day upon taking the first pace. The path keeps to the general level of the two locations and sweeps broad curves around open graded shrub and grassland permitting continuous and unrestricted views over to the left where the appealing scenery is an absolute picture. Almost in continual shadow throughout the day is the northern entrance to the Mont Blanc road tunnel, not now the eyecatching scar it was for the years following its completion in 1965. It has become 'weathered' and although it has toned in with its surroundings, the final approaches of the zig-zagging motorway reaching towards it are beyond disguise.

Snakes are known to frequent the whole of this range, so be extremely cautious and take care not to step on a sunbathing viper. Vipers are timid and will probably scuttle out of harm's way as they become aware of your approach.

This section of path is known as 'Grand Balcon' and it does not take long to realise why it is so called. Fifty-five minutes to the clearing known as **Charlanon** where a path ascending from Chamonix crosses to venture higher in the direction of lac Cornu. At

125

the near end of the clearing is the Pierre à Charlanon, a naturally-gouged stone that has been positioned to retain the water trickling into it from a standpipe. This is as good a bivouac site as any backpacker could require and practically every night sees it being put to good use.

The path cants up slightly as it crosses the clearing but soon levels to continue towards **Plan Praz**. For a short distance, the path has been destroyed by the provision of another ski slope but, once at the head of this, bear R for a moment to regain the path (wider now) which bears L to get to the base of the path ascending to col Brévent, 50mins. Some 2 to 3mins down the slope towards the Plan Praz cableway station there is a bar / restaurant called the 'Restaurant 2000', but no accommodation is available. It is here that you will probably be joined by the trickle of walkers who spent the night in the valley and have come up from Chamonix by bubblecar.

Getting back on course, you will find yourself ascending the narrow path going up the shoulder, indicated: 'Brévent/col du Brévent/Clochetons'. After 20mins take care to turn L off the path which continues to Clochetons. The path twists and wriggles its way upwards, frequently coming to the 'front' end of the shoulder from where exquisite sightings present themselves and the imposing Brévent summit can be seen further along the ridgeline at the top end of the cableway. From the turning it takes an additional 30mins to get to col du Brévent.

The **col du Brévent** is a saddle and rising to it from the other side is the path GR5 coming from the col d'Anterne, which can be seen just to the R of the Pnte d'Anterne, the RH extreme of the Rochers de Fiz. It is a nice place to sit awhile and the gaze will naturally be directed over the Chamonix valley to where the summit of the Aig. du Midi is the central feature, the glacier des Bossons exposing its full drop just to the R.

The path heading towards the Brévent strikes away from the other side of the saddle by first rising slightly and then entering a combe where it drops along the RHS. Exercise care in places where it is necessary to ascend short sections of rocks, but it is not too demanding. From these exposed pitches the 'path' goes along the northern side of the main ridge and so it is possible to get views into the Diosaz valley whilst the Mont Blanc chain is hidden. The final

126

approach to **the Brévent** summit is up a track formed amongst the multitude of large stones that litter the steep slope and whilst it is not particularly comfortable to walk on it doesn't last long. Forty-five minutes from col du Brévent.

You could feel some resentment when finding yourself amongst so many other people on the terrace at Brévent, or perhaps just a little smug because you know you got there by your own efforts, whereas the bulk of the others will have come up by cablecar. You'll quickly be able to see for yourself why so many tourists want to make the excursion as it is such an obviously advantageous spot, the complete panoramic view it affords being revered as one of the best viewing platforms in the Alps. A compensating feature of the cableway's relatively recent re-vamp has been the provision of a good-quality cafeteria which beneficially bolsters the facilities of the shabby little bar that seems to survive unaltered on the viewing terrace.

Revel in the view - Mont Blanc is probably best seen from this vantage point so here it is on display, buttressed by its satellites and seeding several magnificent glaciers. There is a lot of written work describing Mont Blanc as being the 'Monarch of the Alps' whereas other people are content to liken the mountain to an 'enormous cake covered in icing sugar'. Surely it is both these things when seen from the Brévent and much more, depending on the way your imagination can come into play.

From here to les Houches it's *downhill* all the way! Descend from the terraces by the same stony track but watch out for an indistinct junction, where go L. This descends for 10mins or so amongst the stones and then becomes a fine path shooting along to the R, just below the ridge extending from the Brévent. In some 45mins, go L at a path junction taking you onto the LHS of the ridge. The whole of Chamonix is laid out some 1,190m (3,900ft) below like a small Persian carpet. Hang-gliding is the craze hereabouts and they propel themselves off the ridge with a degree of confidence that defies belief and are long out of sight before they reach the valley bottom! The refuge at **Bellachat** is diagonally below and it will take only another 10mins to get to it.

This refuge, 30 places, is relatively new in Alpine terms and is not only delightfully situated but a warm friendliness exudes from the place. It is run by a charming lady who produces the most appetizing snacks with the minimum of delay. The view across the valley is beautifully balanced when seen from here: with such a sight and a good meal who could want for anything more out of life than this?

This is the best place for viewing the glacier des Bossons head-on, as the full display of its tumbling course from head to toe is directly visible. This is reputed to be the only significant glacier in the Alps that is actually growing in length: most others are retracting whilst a few are only managing to 'hold their own'. Another distinction belonging to the Bossons is that it descends to the lowest altitude. If you dwell on the macabre, you may care to know that should an unfortunate climber slip beyond recall into the upper crevasses of the Bossons glacier, then it will take about 45 years before the corpse emerges at the bottom; a measure of its progression. This is on record as having happened. The glacier to the right is the Taconnaz, separated from the Bossons by the long rocky spur of the Montagne de la Côte.

There is a direct path descending to Chamonix from Bel Achat but be careful not to choose this one at the junction. Apart from the one leading to the Brévent there is another heading up for Aiguillette but get onto another path that starts just to the left of this and then drops steeply into a bowl beneath the continuing ridge. This zig-zags violently until levelling to cross the face of the hillside. At some trees, 25mins, you will see for the first time the four buildings comprising the **Merlet** zoo situated at the grassy clearing diagonally below L. Another 27mins to steep hairpins aided by five metal treads and a handrail which descends to negotiate a torrent. Once past this, the path goes through shrubs and then encounters the upper corner of the zoo's boundary fence, 8mins.

Go L down the side of the 10 foot high boundary fence if it is your intention to get access to the zoo, otherwise go R and bear L as it curves down. Once past the fence, cut down L on a wide track to where there is a service entrance for the zoo in the corner of the perimeter wire. A few paces more will bring you on to the road which links the valley to the zoo, 22mins. Turn R and walk down the road for two hundred paces, where look for path entrance on L. The path used to start much nearer to where you come on the road, but avalanches have been responsible for the change: be alert for its possible restoration to its original position as the landscape revives.

The path quickly gets into the woods which remain for the 20mins it takes to get to the unusual concrete statue 'le Christ Roi' in a small clearing on the L. The picnic tables there might encourage one last brew-up before getting to the roadway marking the upper limits of **les Houches.** There is a series of paths going practically all the way down to the vicinity of les Houches station and so there is no need to walk the length of the sweeping hairpins of the road.

So, journey's end! Congratulations will be in order for completing your *Tour of Mont Blanc.*

* * *

As an addendum to the route just described, readers might like to know of an alternative route descending to les Houches from the vicinity of the Bellachat refuge, albeit adding some 2hrs or so to the times already quoted. This goes over the summit of the **l'Aiguillette des Houches,** a 2,285m peak to the west of the saddle just above the refuge. The route is signed, first going diagonally R over a grassy plateau that comprises the saddle (superb views to the north!) and then by gradual ascent up a well-defined path that skirts rocky terrain to the L before swinging to reach the obvious high point. Not a way that would be recommended in bad weather or restricted visibility, but, in the right conditions, the views from the summit are far-reaching and well worth the diversion. The direct descent, though, to les Houches from there might seem never ending but to compensate for the anguish of that you will have the satisfaction of knowing that you have not missed one of the nicest viewpoints in the region.

The Torino Hut is reached by cable-car from la Palud near Courmayeur

Appendix 1:
Time in Courmayeur

APPENDIX 1: TIME IN COURMAYEUR

If you want to stay in Courmayeur for a couple of nights the first game to play is a variation on 'hunt the hotel'. Over the years the cheaper hotels have gradually disappeared and been replaced by more prestigious establishments. There might be the odd bargain to be found by probing the back streets although, in general, cheap accommodation is only to be found elsewhere, such as Entrèves. This one handicap should not prohibit your visit to this charming mountain resort and, once there, you will soon be attracted to its numerous merits. Despite the prices, hotels abound. The restaurants offer a whole range of styles, menus and prices, so there are no complaints in that department.

Courmayeur, 1,220m (4,003ft), is steeped in mountaineering history, with lots of to-ing and fro-ing of healthy-looking young Continentals. There are off-duty (or duty-seeking!) guides with faces the colour and texture of old walnuts. The varied shopping facilities are of the highest standard and even going from shop window to shop window can be an interesting way of spending an hour or so. There is a major Post Office, which is to be found just behind the Tourist Office which faces the coach park next to the motorway turn-off. The coach park doubles as a street market for one day in the week and it then becomes the scene of much bustling activity. Telephoning used to be made possible only by the use of special grooved coins (called *gettone*) but the need to use them has almost been completely overtaken by the plastic card which can be bought at the special telephone office facing the coach park, any tobacconist or the post office. Tobacconists are also official agencies for selling postage stamps. Buses leave here for val Vény, val Ferret, Aosta (a major town lower down the val d'Aosta) and Chamonix.

This town is a suitable place to re-stock portable larders. Perhaps it is also time to make an assessment of the money situation and visit one of the banks. Try not to let ready cash get to too low a level as it is generally uneconomical to cash travellers' cheques at places other than reputable exchange offices. In an emergency some hotels, shops, restaurants and garages offer to change money, but it is impossible to be certain that it is based on the best rate of

131

The Géant (left) peeps over the intervening mountains, whilst the huge Grandes Jorasses dominates on the right of the picture. In the foreground is the hamlet of Dolonne, easily reached from Courmayeur

exchange. A postcard sent from here will stand a sporting chance of beating you home.

PHOTOGRAPHY IN THE ENVIRONS

If you are a keen photographer, consider spending a few leisurely hours in the little village of **Dolonne** where the old buildings, narrow streets and colourful alleyways will undoubtedly be an inspiration. The building styles seem to have remained unchanged over the centuries and despite the advent of modern amenities, some ladies of the village still choose to wash their families' clothes at the communal washing shelters - nothing wrong in that, of course, but an abrupt indication of their ability to withstand a harder way of life. Courmayeur itself is not without photogenic opportunity and a little exploration is all that is necessary to get some enchanting material. **Verrand** is very similar to Dolonne, some 20mins walk from the centre of the town and is reached by continuing along the minor road heading south or by the linking footpath which goes just to the left.

Dolonne is a wonderful old village, full of charm and spectacle. A road links Courmayeur with Dolonne, ducking under the motorway and descending first to an old arch bridge. From the bridge there is a magnificent view of the main range, held, as it were, between the 'V' notch formed by the flanks of Mont Chétif and Monte de la Saxe. The solitary spike of the Dent du Géant heads the skyline at the left-hand end, the ridge of the Arête de Rochefort takes the centre spread, then dipping a little before culminating in the various summits that comprise the Grandes Jorasses at the right.

THE HIGH-LEVEL CABLEWAYS and the TORINO refuge

If for some reason the TMB cannot be continued and there is a need to get back to Chamonix then this is easily accomplished and with the opportunity of doing it in grand style. People only having a week in the area will find this to be the ideal spot to abandon the Tour and by utilizing the high-level cableway will really finish their holiday with something special to remember. A cheaper, quicker, easier and 'less frightening' way of getting to Chamonix is to use the bus service which departs from just outside the tourist office and terminates in the forecourt of Chamonix railway station.

To avail yourself of the stupendous and thrilling cableway experience it is not necessary to go all the way over to Chamonix - and in any case the sequential 6-stage journey will only be continuous if weather conditions are favourable. The lower station of the system is at **la Palud**, slightly higher than Entrèves, at the beginning of val Ferret. The bus from Courmayeur going to la Vachey stops outside. The first cable-car goes up as far as Mont Fréty where an interchange is made for the major ascent to the Torino mountain hotel/restaurant, 3,322m (10,899ft). The mountainside is renowned for the odd herd of chamois that roam its heights, but it takes a sharp eye to spot their progress.

The **Torino** refuge/restaurant is a wonderful place to spend the night and there's possibly no finer spot to witness the sunset and greet the dawn. The restaurant produces substantial lunches and evening meals, the bar operating throughout the day. To get to these

*Dramatic scenery can be seen from the Torino Hut -
the Aiguille Noire de Peuterey*

premises from the cable-car platform it is necessary to climb a very steep stairway which shares a dank rising tunnel with the service hoist. The vista from the Torino terrace is magnificent. The seemingly near at hand Peuterey is difficult to ignore with its spikey ridges continuing up towards the summits of Mont Blanc. The Dent du Géant, (4,013m) (13,166ft), takes on a new importance and this is seen across the enormous intervening icefield where summer skiing continues to link one winter with the next. Then further south beyond Courmayeur lies the heartland of the Gran Paradiso, although only representative sightings can be had of its many glorious summits.

It is possible to go higher still to get to the viewing terrace at **Helbronner**, 3,462m (11,358ft) and cable cabins make easy work of this short distance, although it is possible to go from the Torino refuge to Helbronner by walking over the snowfield. Helbronner's small terrace is truly panoramic, allowing the first unhindered views to the north and showing the continuing cableway heading towards the unmistakable Aig. du Midi over at the far side of the intervening icefields. The Dents du Midi, 3,257m (10,686ft) can be seen to the north and almost due east the characteristic shape of the Matterhorn, 4,478m (14,692ft), which is 60km (37 miles) away. Dropping away from the icefields is the upper section of the Mer de Glace.

There is a busy cafeteria at Helbronner so one could spend a morning there in comfort, just looking, looking, looking. Binoculars are the big aid here, permitting study of detail otherwise unseen. If your intention is to return to la Palud to continue the TMB route then it won't be necessary to proceed further although you might like to contemplate going over to Aig. du Midi, 3,842m (12,605ft), and back just for the pleasure of the ride.

If weather permits, the *télécabine* system should be functioning on its journey high over the great central glaciers to le Gros Rognon and **Aig. du Midi**. This stupendous cable run would be a bargain at any price, but if the weather is perfect and visibility extensive then count yourself amongst the lucky ones and get to the ticket office as quickly as you can. A word of warning: keep an eye on the weather and try to be certain that it will not worsen - don't forget that you have to get back! Passports are needed because Helbronner is also an Italo/Franco frontier post. The cableway trespasses into a land to which it can never rightfully belong, its little bubble-cars daringly hovering hundreds of feet above yawning crevasses that could easily swallow a housing estate without a hint of indigestion. Every so often the cable comes to rest: the operators say this is to 'allow photography' but in reality the halts are to facilitate the passengers at each of the two termini to get in and out of the cabins.

Once at Midi, it is only natural to explore its novelties. The surrounding mountainscape is noticeably different from Helbronner, although the glaring white snow is a common feature. There are different terraces to visit and the view from the bridge linking the two summits is not to be missed - in fact it cannot be missed by those continuing to Chamonix because the upper cableway station is on its northern side. The exit hole used by those descending the ridge for access to the glaciers is worth locating and, if for nothing else, it is usually good for providing a 'framed' photograph of the Aig. Verte.

The cinema and the Alpine Museum in Courmayeur - well, let's hope it's not bad weather that forces you into these.

Appendix 2:
Time in Chamonix

Climbers on the Aiguille du Midi

APPENDIX 2: TIME IN CHAMONIX

The first priority will be to acquire a map of the town from the tourist office. Another helpful publication is a small booklet called *Bienvenue à Chamonix* (Welcome to Chamonix) which lists all the places of interest, giving opening hours, telephone numbers, addresses, etc. They also offer a magnificent walking map called: *Carte des Promenades d'Été en Montagne* (map of summer mountain walks) at some modest charge, which contains valuable and additional information of general interest. The altitude of the town is 1,037m (3,402ft).

Chamonix is a nice enough base to get established: it has so many hotels of different grades from which a sensible choice can be made. There are restaurants which would fulfil the needs of the most discerning and, at the other end of the scale, there is a self-service place where quicker and cheaper meals may be consumed without the formalities associated with the posher places. But why stay in Chamonix? Les Houches has a much quainter character and is linked with Chamonix by a regular bus service (Chamonix bus) and the narrow-gauge railway. But, having arrived at les Houches, why not select a comfortable-looking hotel there and then get along to Chamonix first thing in the morning with a light pack? From all the hotels available, the Auberge le Beau Site (very close to the church in les Houches) with its associated restaurant le Pèle wouldn't disappoint in either regard. Again, there are many other hotels as well as cheaper accommodation from which to choose in addition to a couple of good camp sites.

As for Chamonix itself, the hotel la Roma is a very practical place in which to stay: the only meal provided is breakfast and their comfortable rooms mostly have a built-in shower in addition to the H&C washbasin. It is run by a particularly friendly family, the proprietor speaks English and the charges are competitive. The Roma is on the outskirts of town in the direction of les Houches along the route de Genève (continuation of rue Dr. Paccard from the centre of Chamonix). There is an *auberge de jeunesse* (youth hostel) in addition to some twenty-odd camping sites littering the length of the valley floor, several within close proximity of Chamonix, but for up-to-date detail it would be better to consult the *Bienvenue à Chamonix* booklet.

Excursion to AIGUILLE du MIDI

This could well be the highlight of the holiday. The base station is fairly close to the centre of **Chamonix** (let the eye follow the line of the cable to pinpoint the place!). It is generally good advice to get onto one of the earlier cable-car departures because visibility generally becomes poorer around midday. Whilst there can be no guarantee of clarity, the morning usually holds the best prospect. The cable-car soon flits up to the intermediate station at **Plan l'Aiguille**, 2,310m (7,579ft), which is above the tree-line on a broad rocky shoulder. In moments, transfer is made to another car which completes the journey by the dizzy suspension line high above the Pélerins glacier to reach the upper station at **Aiguille du Midi**, 3,795m (12,451ft). The cable has no intermediate supports and its catenary is about 2,900m (9,500ft) in length. Icicles formed overnight on the suspension cable can reach a surprising length and these are snapped off as the first car of the day runs past, falling onto the roof with frightening impact.

This prince of viewpoints is no longer the prerogative of the climber - thanks to the way the cable engineer has exercised his talents with breathtaking daring. The majesty that feasts the eyes from the Midi's renowned terraces is difficult to comprehend, let alone describe. Surely the most glorious view is that towards the glacier de Talèfre which is flanked by Verte on its left and the north wall of the Jorasses to the right. Once more the Matterhorn can be seen, to the immediate right of the nearer Gd. Combin. Sharing the skyline way in the distance is the rounded hump of Monte Rosa.

Swinging the gaze completely to the right, Mont Blanc seems remarkably near, although it is 6km (3¹/₂ miles) away. The view over the upper section of the Bossons glacier is awesome, its great rucked surface poised menacingly. Buildings in the Chamonix valley, far below, are only just recognizable. From such a height, the roads look just like threads of cotton and are only brought alive by the insect-like vehicles crawling along them. Binoculars are a wonderful aid to increasing pleasures at Midi - they show a whole variety of ski parties and climbing groups that would otherwise remain unseen.

The best will probably have been seen by noon and if you are leaving about then it is suggested that the returning cable-car be taken only as far as **Plan l'Aiguille**, where 15mins away - almost hidden - is the delightful Chalet-Refuge du Plan which is well worth considering for taking lunch (dortoirs available).

MONTENVERS

After leaving the chalet the resumption of the cableway descent is the obvious way of getting from **Plan l'Aiguille** to Chamonix but there is an alternative that will absorb the remaining hours of the afternoon and this takes in a visit to one of the oldest mountain venues of the area - Montenvers, 1,914m (6,279ft). To get to Montenvers from Plan take the horizontal path in the NE direction which becomes another 'balcony' route, offering unhampered views over Chamonix towards the Aiguilles Rouges. It is an easy path, too. After about 1hr 30mins there is a choice of continuing straight ahead or branching up a steep track to the right: take the zig-zags. This climbs to the head of a brow where there is a defile strewn with loose slate, evoking memories of untidy Welsh quarries. As the route slopes downwards the Mer de Glace can be seen, with the café terrace of the **Montenvers** appearing as a spot just above it. With calf-high thickets, the path finally curves down towards the touristy rail-head.

Mingling with the crowd will have little attraction after having had the 'freedom of the hills' for the preceding couple of hours, but the place does offer an attractive aspect of Grandes Jorasses' legendary north wall and the stupendous face of the Dru directly across the glacier. (Iron ladders descended to the glacier to enable tourists to visit 'ice caves', but these collapsed in late 1987 and may not have been replaced.)

The majority of the other visitors will return to the valley by rail, but surely the old mule path will be your choice in preference to the train? This is one of the oldest of mountain tracks, probably trodden by millions over the years. One of the most popular mountain views - featured in many French tourist office publicity brochures - is of the Dru, 3,733m (12,247ft), seen above the S-shape railway viaduct

*The great north face of the Grandes Jorasses looks very impressive from the
Aiguille du Midi*

which can be found shortly after leaving Montenvers.

The railway line is crossed more than once but take special care at one spot where the danger is not so much from trains but by the strong possibility of taking the wrong path and reaching the valley several kilometres off target. The proper path is hidden behind a stout building next to the line, so don't miss it. Overcoming this particular snag, the pleasant, forest-covered path reaches habitation adjacent to the railway station at Chamonix and it will take just over the hour to complete the descent by this means.

Don't be tempted to go right up to Midi if the weather is gloomy or if the summit station and terraces are in cloud as it would be a complete waste of money and in all probability uncomfortably chilly. Far better to wait for another occasion. The ticket office staff should be able to tell you what the conditions are likely to be at the top.

LAC des GAILLANDS

This lake is really beautiful in its setting and to visit it will absorb half a day at most. Walk in the general direction of les Houches from Chamonix by way of the rue Dr. Paccard and the continuing route de Genève. This is the old road plying the valley and has little traffic now that the motorway bears the brunt. The **lac des Gaillands** is another traditional photography stance - cynics say that they can see the tripod holes! It makes a wonderful picture which includes the major summits and ridges leading up to Mont Blanc as they pile height upon height above the dark trees that line the far side of the water. The building at the end of the lake is the Pélerins railway station.

Right next to the near end of the lake is a rock wall which features the *École d'Escalation* (climbing school) and on a busy morning there are sometimes a hundred beginners in various stages of progression up its face, responding to a cackle of instructions from below. Going through the adjacent woods which start at the rocks will bring you onto the roadway near les Bossons: 30mins along an attractive wooded path, passing a mysterious haunted-looking folly building of which nobody seems to know the history. The reason for going to **les Bossons**, a nice little village in itself, is

The Gaillands rocks near Chamonix are used by climbers
(Photo: R.B.Evans)

143

to cross the motorway and get up the narrow lane opposite which leads to the chair-lift system for the glacier. It is easy to walk up to the head of the chair-lift cables from where it is possible to venture through a gap and get right down to the tongue of the **Bossons glacier**. Novices are usually undergoing instruction in the techniques associated with glacier work and whilst this is relatively fascinating to observe, the main attraction will be the enormity of the spectacular glistening snout.

THE TOWN

Chamonix's shops will undoubtedly attract and a pleasant hour or so can be spent ferreting around its interesting streets. There are several photographic shops which display superb ready-made prints, all with mountain scenery as the theme, most of which are for sale. Dozens of cafés and bars. Several *crêperies* (pancake shops). Cream cakes threaten the waistline. Then there are the climbing-gear shops, extremely interesting knick-knack displays, sensibly-stocked supermarkets, fruiterers, bakers, clothing shops. Take your life in your hands and order a *Glâce Meringue Chantilly* with a coffee at one of the pavement cafés!

Most walkers might appreciate having the Caféteria le Grillandin brought to their attention. This is a self-service restaurant that is open every day. It displays a wide selection and at prices which seem to be within the pockets of all. This little haven is to be found in rue J. Vallot.

A few doors along from the centrally-situated Post Office (PTT) will be found the legendary **Bar National**. Affectionately known as the *'Bar Nash'*, it is a popular haunt for American and British climbers and one of the best rendezvous points in the locality.

ACCOMMODATION DIRECTORY

Accommodation abounds in the main places like les Houches, les Contamines, Courmayeur, Champex, Chamonix and its valley spread. At places round the general route of the TMB there is, naturally, less choice and the opportunity is taken to list those that are appropriate along with detail of economic refuge-style places in the above-named places.

Note that the information will be given in the order of its location, the name of the establishment (with address if located in a conurbation), the telephone number, dates of opening, number of places in dortoir (D), number of places in bedrooms (B). All this is as per that available at the time of going to print and it would be naïve to believe that these would continue into ensuing years without some modification, so normal disclaimers must apply. As has been mentioned earlier in the text, lists of accommodation can be obtained by application to the Tourist Offices and Syndicat d'Initiative offices in the region.

FRANCE

les Houches - Chalet CIALC, les Granges - 04 50 54 41 81 15.06 to 15.09 - 20B - must be reserved

les Houches - Chalet Aiguille du Midi, Av. des Alpages 04 50 55 50 36 - 15.12 to 01.09 - 6D 40B

les Houches - Refuge le Crêt - 04 50 55 52 27 - all year - 10D 9B

col de Voza - Hôtel de la Prarion - 04 50 54 40 07 26.06 to 25.09 -12D 19B

Bionnassay - Auberge de Bionnassay - 04 50 93 45 23 25.12 to 02.11 - 15D 17B

Miage - Refuge de Miage - 04 50 93 22 91 01.06 to 30.09 - 30D

Truc - Auberge du Truc - 04 50 93 12 48 - 18.06 to 10.09 - 28D

les Contamines - Refuge du C.A.F. (Club Alpin Française), 22 Rte du Plan du Moulin - 04 50 47 00 88 - 15.06 to 30.09 - 28D - must be reserved les Contamines - la Roselette - 04 50 47 13 31 early 06 to end 10 - 25D

towards N.D. de la Gorge - Gîte d'Étape du Pontet - 04 50 47 04 04
13.05 to 30.09 - 30D - must be reserved

Nant-Borrant - Refuge Nant-Borrant - 04 50 47 03 57 15.06 to end 09
- 35D

la Balme - Chalet la Balme - 04 50 47 03 54 15.06 to 15.09 - 36D 14B
- must be reserved

Croix du Bonhomme - Refuge de la Croix du Bonhomme - 04 79 07
05 28 15.06 to 20.09 - 113D

les Chapieux - Auberge de la Nova - 04 79 89 07 15 15.05 to 30.10 -
35D 30B - must be reserved

Mottets - Refuge des Mottets - 04 79 07 01 70 21.06 to 10.09 - 50D

ITALY

Elisabetta - Refuge Elisabetta - 0165 84 40 80 15.06 to 15.09 - 60D 20B

Chécrouit - Maison Vielle - 0337 23 09 79 - 15.06 to 25.09 - 30D

below Chécrouit - Refuge Monte Bianco - 0165 86 90 97 18.06 to 19.09
- 12D 54B

la Palud - Hotel de la Funivia - 0165 899 24 (?) 06.06 to 30.09 - 32D 20B

la Saxe - Refuge Bertone - 0165 84 46 12 - 15.06 to 25.09 - 45D 5B

Lavachey - Hotel Lavachey - 0165 86 97 23 - 18.06 to 26.09 - 26B

Arnuva - no detail available, but information to author that limited
accommodation available

Pré de Bar - Refuge Elena - 0165 84 46 88 - 15.06 to 15.09 -114D 13B

SWITZERLAND

la Ferret - Hôtel de Ferret - 27 783 11 80 01.04. to 30.06 (?) - 30B

la Ferret - Hôtel du col de Fenêtre - 27 783 11 88 01.06 to 10.09 - 26D
14B

la Fouly - Hôtel des Glaciers - 27 783 11 71 - all year 34D 22B

la Fouly - Hôtel Edelweiss - 27 783 26 21 - 01.06 to 31.10 - 30D 22B la Fouly - Refuge le Dolent - 27 783 18 63 - all year - 70D 11B - must be reserved

la Fouly - Camping des Glaciers - 27 783 17 35 01.06 to 30.09 - 28D (in tented dortoir) which must be reserved, in addition to general camping

la Fouly - Chalet les Girolles - 27 783 18 75 - all year - 60B

Orny - Cabane d'Orny - detail not known but estimated to hold about 60D

Plâteau du Trient - Cabane du Trient - detail not known but estimated to hold about 70D

Champex - Au Club Alpin - 27 783 11 61 - 26.12 to 15.11 25D - must be reserved

Champex - Relais le Belvédère - 27 783 11 14 - all year - 20B

Champex - Chalet En Plein Air - 27 783 23 50 - all year - 36D 25B

Champex - Auberge de la Fôret - 27 783 12 78 - all year - 15D

Arpette - Relais d'Arpette - 27 783 12 21 01.06 to 15.10 - 70D 10B - must be reserved

Forclaz - Hôtel du Col de la Forclaz - 27 722 26 88 - all year - 40D 35B

Trient - Refuge de Peuty - 79 219 14 48 - 15.06 to 15.09 - 37D

Trient - Relais du Mont Blanc - 27 722 46 23 - all year - 60D 16B - must be reserved

Trient - Cafe-Gîte Moret - 27 722 27 07 - all year - 13B

Balme - Refuge de Col de Balme - detail not known but estimated to hold about 40D

FRANCE

Albert Premier - detail not known but estimated to hold about 60D

le Tour - Chalet Alpin du Tour (CAF) - 04 50 54 04 16 01.04 to 19.09 - 83D 4B

Montroc - Gîte d'Étape du Moulin - 04 50 54 05 37 15.12 to 30.09 - 38D

Trelechamps - Gîte d'Étape la Boerne - 04 50 54 05 14 10.12 to 10.11 - 32D

Argentiere - le Vieux Grassonnet - 04 50 54 12 27 01.07 to 30.09 -16D 4B

lac Blanc - Refuge lac Blanc - 04 50 47 24 49 - 30D - span of opening not known: probably end of June to beginning of September

la Flégère - Refuge la Flégère - 04 50 53 06 13 12.06 to 19.09 - 66D 19B - must be reserved

Bellachat - Refuge Bellachat - 04 50 53 43 23 25.06 to 15.09 - 28D

Chamonix - Auberge de Jeunesse (youth hostel) du Mont Blanc, 127 Montée Jaques Balmat - 04 50 53 14 52 - 01.12 to 01.10 - 120B

Chamonix - Chalet Ski Station, 6 Rte des Moussoux - 04 50 53 20 25 26.06 to 19.09 - 57D

Chamonix - le Chamoniard Volant, 45 Rte de la Frasse - 04 50 53 14 09 - all year - 70D

*   *   *   *

The author expresses his gratitude to the staff of the Office de Tourisme at les Contamines for providing the detail of this useful Directory and for giving their permission for its inclusion.

CICERONE GUIDE BOOKS
LONG DISTANCE WALKS

There are many Cicerone guides to long distance walks in Britain or abroad, which make a memorable holiday or shorter break.

GENERAL TREKKING

THE TREKKER'S HANDBOOK Thomas R. Gilchrist Everything a trekker needs to know, from gear to health. *ISBN 1 85284 205 9 A5 size*

FAR HORIZONS Adventure Travel for All! Walt Unsworth From European trails to Himalayan treks; from deserts of Central Asia to jungles of Borneo; from wildwater rafting to gorges of the Yangtse. Based on the author's wide experience of this growing form of holiday travel. *ISBN 1 85284 228 8 160pp A5 size*

LAKE DISTRICT & NORTHERN ENGLAND

THE CUMBRIA WAY AND ALLERDALE RAMBLE Jim Watson. A guide to two popular Lake District long distance walks. *ISBN 1 85284 242 3*

THE EDEN WAY Charlie Emett Through a romantic part of Cumbria. Breaks into sections by using the popular Settle-Carlisle railway. *ISBN 1 85284 040 4 192pp*

IN SEARCH OF WESTMORLAND Charlie Emett A walk around the old county. Full of rich anecdotes and history. *ISBN 0 902363 66 2 200pp*

WALKING ROUND THE LAKES John & Anne Nuttall The ideal walk encompassing all the major summits, yet with high and low level alternatives. *ISBN 1 85284 099 4 240pp*

WESTMORLAND HERITAGE WALK Chris Wright and Mark Richards A circular walk around the old county. *ISBN 0 902363 94 8 256pp PVC cover*

THE DALES WAY Terry Marsh A practical handbook to a very popular walk. With Accommodation Guide. *ISBN 1 85284 102 8 136pp*

THE DOUGLAS VALLEY WAY Gladys Sellers Through the heart of Lancashire. *ISBN 1 85284 073 0 72pp*

HADRIAN'S WALL Vol 1: The Wall Walk Mark Richards Mark conducts you along the wall, accompanied by his skilful maps and sketches. *ISBN 1 85284 128 1 224pp*

THE ISLE OF MAN COASTAL PATH Aileen Evans The Raad ny Foillan path encircles the island; the Herring Way and the Millennium Way are also described. *ISBN 0 902363 95 6 144pp*

LAUGHS ALONG THE PENNINE WAY Pete Bogg Anyone who has struggled through the bogs of the Pennine Way will identify with the humour of this cartoon book. An ideal gift. *ISBN 0 902363 97 2 104pp*

A NORTHERN COAST TO COAST WALK Terry Marsh The most popular LD walk in Britain. Includes accommodation guide. *ISBN 1 85284 126 5 280pp £7.99*

THE RIBBLE WAY Gladys Sellers From sea to source close to a junction with the Pennine Way. *ISBN 1 85284 107 9 112pp*

THE REIVER'S WAY James Roberts 150 miles around Northumberland. *ISBN 1 85284 130 3 112pp*

THE TEESDALE WAY Martin Collins A new walk which follows the Tees from its source to the sea. 100 miles, 8 stages. *ISBN 1 85284 198 2 112pp*

WALKING THE CLEVELAND WAY & THE MISSING LINK Malcolm Boyes Circular tour of the North York Moors, including some of our finest coastline. *ISBN 1 85284 014 5 144pp*

WHITE PEAK WAY Robert Haslam An 80-mile walk through the Derbyshire Dales with full details of youth hostels, pubs etc. *ISBN 1 85284 056 0 96pp*

WEEKEND WALKS IN THE PEAK DISTRICT John & Anne Nuttall Magnificent weekend outings illustrated with John's fine drawings. *ISBN 1 85284 137 0 296pp*

THE VIKING WAY John Stead From Barton-upon-Humber to Rutland Water. *ISBN 1 85284 057 9 172pp*

WALES & THE WELSH BORDER

THE LLEYN PENINSULA COASTAL PATH John Cantrell. Starting at Caernarfon the coastal path goes round the peninsula to Porthmadog following the old Bardsey Pilgrims' route. Described for walkers and cyclists, with additional day walks. *ISBN 1 85284 252 0*

WALKING OFFA'S DYKE PATH David Hunter Along the Welsh Marches, 170 miles from Chepstow to Prestatyn. *ISBN 1 85284 160 5 224pp*

THE PEMBROKESHIRE COASTAL PATH Dennis R. Kelsall One of Britain's most beautiful paths. includes accommodation guide. *ISBN 1 85284 186 9 200pp*

SARN HELEN Arthur Rylance & John Cantrell The length of Wales in the footsteps of the Roman legions. *ISBN 1 85284 101 X 248pp*

WALKING DOWN THE WYE David Hunter 112 mile walk from Rhayader to Chepstow. *ISBN 1 85284 105 2 192pp*

A WELSH COAST TO COAST WALK- Snowdonia to Gower John Gillham An ideal route for backpackers, away from waymarked trails. *ISBN 1 85284 218 0 152pp*

SOUTHERN ENGLAND

THE COTSWOLD WAY Kev Reynolds A guide to this popular walk. *ISBN 1 85284 049 8 168pp*

THE GRAND UNION CANAL WALK Clive Holmes Along the canal which links the Black Country to London, through rural England *ISBN 1 85284 206 7 128pp*

THE KENNET & AVON WALK Ray Quinlan 90 miles along riverside and canal, from Westminster to Avonmouth, full of history, wildlife, delectable villages and pubs. *ISBN 1 85284 090 0 200pp*

AN OXBRIDGE WALK J.A.Lyons Over 100 miles linking the university cities of Oxford and Cambridge. *ISBN 1 85284 166 4 168pp*

THE SOUTHERN COAST-TO-COAST WALK *Ray Quinlan* The equivalent of the popular northern walk. 283 miles from Weston-super-Mare to Dover. *ISBN 1 85284 117 6 200pp*

THE SOUTH DOWNS WAY & THE DOWNS LINK *Kev Reynolds* A guide to these popular walks. *ISBN 1 85284 023 4 136pp*

SOUTH WEST WAY - A Walker's Guide to the Coast Path Vol.1 Minehead to Penzance *Martin Collins ISBN 1 85284 025 0 184pp PVC cover*

Vol.2 Penzance to Poole *Martin Collins ISBN 1 85284 026 9 198pp PVC cover*

Two volumes which cover the spectacular coastal path around Britain's south-west peninsula.

THE TWO MOORS WAY *James Roberts* 100 miles crossing Dartmoor, the villages of central Devon and Exmoor to the coast at Lynmouth. *ISBN 1 85284 159 1 100pp*

THE WEALDWAY & THE VANGUARD WAY *Kev Reynolds* Two LD walks in Kent, from the outskirts of London to the coast. *ISBN 0 902363 85 9 160pp*

SCOTLAND

THE WEST HIGHLAND WAY *Terry Marsh* A practical guide to this very popular walk. *ISBN 1 85284 235 0*

IRELAND

THE IRISH COAST TO COAST WALK *Paddy Dillon* From Dublin and the Wicklows to Valencia Island on the Kerry coast, linking various trails. *ISBN 1 85284 211 3*

FRANCE

THE BRITTANY COASTAL PATH *Alan Castle* The GR34, 360 miles takes a month to walk. Easy access from UK means it can be split into several holidays. *ISBN 1 85284 185 0 296pp*

THE CORSICAN HIGH LEVEL ROUTE - Walking the GR20 *Alan Castle* The most challenging of the French LD paths - across the rocky spine of Corsica. *ISBN 1 85284 100 1 104pp*

THE PYRENEAN TRAIL: GR10 *Alan Castle* From the Atlantic to the Mediterranean at a lower level than the Pyrenean High Route. 50 days but splits into holiday sections. *ISBN 1 85284 245 8 176pp*

THE ROBERT LOUIS STEVENSON TRAIL *Alan Castle* 140 mile trail in the footsteps of Stevenson's "Travels with a Donkey" through the Cevennes. *ISBN 1 85284 060 9 160pp*

TOUR OF MONT BLANC *Andrew Harper* One of the world's best walks - the circumnavigation of the Mont Blanc massif. *ISBN 1 85284 240 7 168pp PVC cover*

TOUR OF THE OISANS: GR54 *Andrew Harper* Around the massif, similar in quality to the Tour of Mont Blanc. *ISBN 1 85284 157 5 120pp PVC cover*

THE TOUR OF THE QUEYRAS *Alan Castle* 13 days across the sunniest part of the French Alps. Suitable for a first Alpine visit. *ISBN 1 85284 048 X 160pp*

TOUR OF THE VANOISE *Kev Reynolds* A circuit of one of the finest mountain areas of France. The second most popular mountain tour after the Tour of Mont Blanc. *ISBN*

150

1 85284 224 5 120pp

WALKING THE FRENCH ALPS: GR5 *Martin Collins* The popular From Lake Geneva to Nice. Split into stages, each of which could form the basis of a good holiday. *ISBN 1 85284 051 X 160pp*

WALKING THE FRENCH GORGES *Alan Castle* 320 miles through Provence and Ardèche, includes the famous Verdon. *ISBN 1 85284 114 1 224pp*

WALKING IN THE TARENTAISE & BEAUFORTAIN ALPS *J.W. Akitt* Delectable mountains south of Mont Blanc includes the Vanoise National Park. 53 day walks, 5 tours between 2 and 8 days duration, plus 40 short outings. *ISBN 1 85284 181 8 216pp*

WALKS IN VOLCANO COUNTRY *Alan Castle* Two LD walks in Central France- the High Auvergne and Tour of the Velay - in a unique landscape of extinct volcanoes. *ISBN 1 85284 092 7 200pp*

THE WAY OF ST JAMES: GR65 *H.Bishop* French section of the pilgrim's route, across Massif Central from Le Puy to the Pyrenees. *ISBN 1 85284 029 3 96pp*

FRANCE/SPAIN

WALKS & CLIMBS IN THE PYRENEES *Kev Reynolds* Includes the Pyrenean High Level Route.. (3rd Edition) *ISBN 1 85284 133 8 328pp PVC cover*

SPAIN

WALKING IN MALLORCA *June Parker.* The 3rd edition takes account of rapidly changing conditions. Includes the classic multi-day walk through the backbone of the mountains. One of the great walking guides. *ISBN 1 85284 250 4*

THE MOUNTAINS OF CENTRAL SPAIN *Jaqueline Oglesby* Walks and scrambles in the Sierras de Gredos and Guadarrama which rise to 2600m and are snow capped for five months of the year. *ISBN 1 85284 203 2 312p*

THROUGH THE SPANISH PYRENEES: GR11 *Paul Lucia* A new long distance trail which mirrors the French GR10 but traverses much lonelier, wilder country *ISBN 1 85284 222 9 216pp*

WALKING IN THE SIERRA NEVADA *Andy Walmsley* Spain's highest mountain range, a wonderland for traveller and wilderness backpacker. Mountain bike routes are indicated. *ISBN 1 85284 194 X 160pp*

THE WAY OF ST JAMES: SPAIN *Alison Raju* The popular Pilgrim Road from the Pyrenees to Santiago de Compostela. *ISBN 1 85284 142 7 152pp*

SWITZERLAND including adjacent parts of France and Italy

ALPINE PASS ROUTE, SWITZERLAND *Kev Reynolds* Over 15 passes along the northern edge of the Alps, past the Eiger, Jungfrau and many other renowned peaks. *ISBN 1 85284 069 2 176pp*

CHAMONIX to ZERMATT The Walker's Haute Route *Kev Reynolds* In the shadow of great peaks from Mont Blanc to the Matterhorn. *ISBN 1 85284 215 6 176pp*

THE JURA: WALKING THE HIGH ROUTE *Kev Reynolds* **WINTER SKI TRAVERSES** *R.Brian Evans* The High

Route is a LD path along the highest crest of the Swiss Jura. In winter the area is a paradise for cross-country skiers. *ISBN 1 85284 010 2 192pp*

THE GRAND TOUR OF MONTE ROSA *C.J.Wright*
Vol 1 - Martigny to Valle della Sesia (via the Italian valleys) *ISBN 1 85284 177 X 216pp*
Vol 2 - Valle della Sesia to Martigny (via the Swiss valleys) *ISBN 1 85284 178 8 182pp* The ultimate alpine LD walk which encircles most of the Pennine Alps.

GERMANY, AUSTRIA & EASTERN EUROPE

GERMANY'S ROMANTIC ROAD A guide for walkers and cyclists *Gordon McLachlan* 423km past historic walled towns and castles of southern Germany . *ISBN 1 85284 233 4 208pp*

HUT TO HUT IN THE STUBAI ALPS *Allan Hartley* Two classic tours: The Stubai Rucksack Route and The Stubai Glacier Tour, each taking around 10 days. Easy peaks and good huts make it a good area for a first Alpine season. *ISBN 1 85284 123 0 128pp Card cover*

KING LUDWIG WAY *Fleur and Colin Speakman* Travels the Bavarian countryside from Munich to Füssen. King Ludwig was responsible for the fabulous castle of Neuschwanstein *ISBN 0 902363 90 5 80pp*

MOUNTAIN WALKING IN AUSTRIA   *Cecil Davies* Describes walks in 17 mountain groups, from single day to multi-day hut to hut excursions. *ISBN 1 85284 239 3 200pp*

WALKING THE RIVER RHINE TRAIL   *Alan Castle* Along Germany's most famous river.. *ISBN 1 85284 276 8 182pp*

WALKING IN THE BLACK FOREST   *Fleur & Colin Speakman*   Above the Rhine valley, the Westweg was Europe's first waymarked trail in 1900. *ISBN 1 85284 050 1 120pp*

SCANDINAVIA

WALKING IN NORWAY *Connie Roos* 20 walking routes in the main mountain areas from the far south to the sub arctic regions, all accessible by public transport. *ISBN 1 85284 230 X 200pp*

ITALY & SLOVENIA

ALTA VIA - HIGH LEVEL WALKS IN THE DOLOMITES *Martin Collins* A guide to some of the most popular mountain paths in Europe - Alta Via 1 and 2. *ISBN 0 902363 75 1 160pp PVC cover*

THE GRAND TOUR OF MONTE ROSA *C.J.Wright*
See entry under Switzerland

LONG DISTANCE WALKS IN THE GRAN PARADISO *J.W. Akitt.* Describes Alta Via 2 and the Grand Traverse of Gran Paradiso. *ISBN 1 85284 247 4*

MEDITERRANEAN COUNTRIES

THE ATLAS MOUNTAINS *Karl Smith* Trekking in the mountains of north Africa. Practical and comprehensive. *ISBN 1 85284 032 3 136pp PVC cover*

THE MOUNTAINS OF GREECE. A Walker's Guide *Tim Salmon* Hikes of all grades from a month-long traverse of the Pindos to day hikes on the outskirts of Athens. *ISBN 1 85284 108 7 PVC cover*

THE MOUNTAINS OF TURKEY *Karl Smith* Over 100 treks and scrambles with detailed descriptions of all the popular peaks. Includes Ararat. *ISBN 1 85284 161 3 184pp PVC cover*

TREKS AND CLIMBS in WADI RUM, JORDAN *Tony Howard.* The world's foremost desert climbing and trekking area *ISBN 1 85284 135 4   252pp A5 Card cover*

THE ALA DAG, Climbs and Treks in Turkey's Crimson Mountains *O.B.Tüzel.* The best mountaineering area in Turkey. *ISBN 1 85284 112 5   296pp PVC cover*

HIMALAYA

ANNAPURNA - A Trekker's Guide *Kev Reynolds* Includes Annapurna Circuit, Annapurna Sanctuary and Pilgrim's Trail, with lots of good advice. *ISBN 1 85284 132 X 184pp*

EVEREST - A Trekker's Guide *Kev Reynolds* The most popular trekking region in the Himalaya. Lodges, teahouse, permits, health - all are dealt with in this indispensible guide. *ISBN 1 85284 187 7*

LANGTANG, GOSAINKUND & HELAMBU - A Trekker's Guide *Kev Reynolds* Popular area, easily accessible from Kathmandu. *ISBN 1 85284 207 5*

ADVENTURE TREKS IN NEPAL *Bill O'Connor*
ISBN 1 85223 306 0 160pp large format

OTHER COUNTRIES

MOUNTAIN WALKING IN AFRICA 1: KENYA *David Else.* Detailed route descriptions and practical information. *ISBN 1 85365 205 9 180pp A5 size*

TREKKING IN THE CAUCAUSUS *Yuri Kolomiets & Aleksey Solovyev.* Hidden until recently behind the Iron Curtain. Included are the highest tops in Europe, the summits of Mt Elbrus. *ISBN 1 85284 129 X 224pp PVC cover*

ADVENTURE TREKS WESTERN NORTH AMERICA *Chris Townsend.* *ISBN 1 85223 317 6 160pp large format*

CLASSIC TRAMPS IN NEW ZEALAND *Constance Roos.* The 14 best long distance walks in both South and North Islands. *ISBN 1 85284 118 4   208pp PVC cover*

Send for complete Price List of over 270 books - walking, trekking, climbing etc.

Available from all good outdoor shops, bookshops or direct (include P&P) from **Cicerone Press, 2 Police Square, Milnthorpe, Cumbria LA7 7PY.**
Tel: 01539 562069 Fax: 01539 563417
E-mail: info@cicerone.demon.co.uk
Web site: www.cicerone.co.uk

Printed by Carnmor Print & Design, London Road, Preston, Lancashire, England

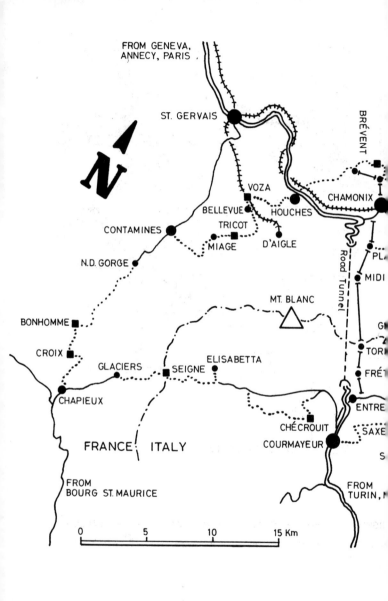